Early American Classics

EARLY AMERICAN CLASSICS

33 BASIC PROJECTS FOR WOODWORKERS, WITH COMPLETE PLANS AND INSTRUCTIONS

JOHN A. NELSON

STACKPOLE
BOOKS

Published by
STACKPOLE BOOKS
Cameron and Kelker Streets
P.O. Box 1831
Harrisburg, PA 17105

The plans for Child's Rocking Chair, English Pipe Box, Hooded Cradle, and Child's Sled are reprinted with permission from *Early American Life*, a publication of Cowles Magazines, Inc., Harrisburg, Pennsylvania.

Printed in the United States of America

First Edition

10 9 8 7 6 5 4 3 2 1

Cover photo by Debbie Porter Hayes
Cover design by Mark B. Olszewski

To my grandson, Daniel John O'Rourke, who was born the same week I finished this book, 18 February 1991.

Library of Congress Cataloging-in-Publication Data

Nelson, John A., 1935—
    Early American classics : 33 projects for woodworkers / John A. Nelson. — 1st ed.
        p.   cm.
    ISBN 0-8117-2535-9
    1. Woodwork.   I. Title.
TT180.N47   1992
749.214—dc20   91-47001
                                                                              CIP

CONTENTS

PREFACE

This book will guide woodworkers in reproducing authentic-looking copies of primitive, colonial, and Early American pieces. But more important, it provides an accurate record of those wonderfully unusual and unique small objects that were so important to the Americans who used them long ago.

Each project in this book is an exact copy of an authentic antique found throughout New England and the northeastern section of this country—right down to the sometimes unusual construction techniques used. No attempt has been made to improve upon the original construction methods by using tools or methods available today. Whenever known, the kind of wood that was used on the original piece is indicated. If the original piece was painted, its original color and details are also given in as much detail as possible in order that the copy be as close to the original as possible. The chapter on finishing and staining explains how to apply a finish that will look like the 150-year-old original.

Every project reproduces a one-of-a-kind antique, probably made by hand and in many cases by a not-so-skilled craftsperson. Each was made to serve a particular, important need in days past. Today that original need has probably changed or become obsolete, but the projects can still be functional.

Most projects throughout this book have been chosen so that only basic woodworking tools are necessary: The craftsperson with very limited space or only basic tools can make the most of them. A lathe is not necessary except to make a few drawer pulls or wooden knobs. If you don't have a lathe, you can buy wooden knobs and drawer pulls very close to the original style from one of the many supply houses listed at the end of this book. River Bend Turning will custom-make other turnings.

This room, from a family dwelling in the Shaker community (1818–1840) of New Lebanon, New York, demonstrates the simple, utilitarian beauty of early American furniture. *(Courtesy of H. Richard Dietrich, Jr., the Philadelphia Museum of Art.)*

Because each reader is at a different skill level and will have different tools, only very brief and basic instructions are given on how to make each of these reproductions. Most projects are simple and should be easy to make in a few hours or over a weekend. Before starting work on any project in this book, however, carefully study the drawings so that you fully understand how it is to be made and assembled. The exploded view provided with each project will illustrate the exact assembly.

I hope you will enjoy making and living with these pieces and that this book will provide you with a way to acquire an interesting, one-of-a-kind collection of Americana that will add warmth to your home for generations to come. I also hope that by making some of these simple projects, beginning woodworkers will gain the confidence to attempt the more advanced projects found in other books and in magazines.

Most photographs of the projects are of new "antiques," but a few are pictures of the originals. Each new project has been made to look as old as the original.

Some of the basic material in the first pages has been taken from my book *Country Classics* because the information and the illustrations are the same.

If you like these projects, you might want to purchase *Colonial Classics* and *Country Classics*, which are also published by Stackpole Books. Any comments from those using this book will be most welcome.

Special appreciation and thanks go to my wife, Joyce, for making sense of my scribblings and notes and for typing them into something sensible. Thanks also to my good friends Jerry Ernce, who got me started in woodworking, and Bill Bigelow, for being my mentor and adviser throughout this book. Thanks, of course, to the many antiques dealers, flea market merchants, and friends throughout New England who allowed me to study, measure, and photograph their wonderful, one-of-a-kind antiques, and to the staff at Stackpole Books for making my rough material into a finished book. Sally Atwater and Sylvia Frank worked especially hard to put this book together. And I would especially like to thank Deborah Porter of Hancock, New Hampshire, for the very fine photographs that captured each "antique" just right. Without the help of these people, this book could not have been completed.

John A. Nelson
Peterborough, New Hampshire
1992

Early Furniture and Accessories

The early settlers brought with them little but tradition when they began settling the new land. They had to begin by building their own homes—and, of course, the furnishings they absolutely needed. Most early settlers had few and meager tools to work with; many had limited building skills. The homes and furnishings they produced were by necessity crude or "primitive"—a term that is applied to many of those early pieces today. This book contains many such primitives: It is a unique style well worth reproducing.

Material was one problem the early settlers didn't have. Wood was abundant: Early settlers worked with first-cut timber from fully matured forests. European craftsmen of that time must have been as envious of the settlers as we are today for the prime timber supply available to them. These trees had been growing for well over one hundred years. The wood was straight grained, tough, clear, and free from defects, reaching widths almost impossible to find today. Ironically, in those days narrow boards were more desired than wide because it was more difficult to rip wood to size. Older houses can be found with narrow floorboards in the living room and boards over 24 inches wide in the attic.

In New Hampshire it is not uncommon to find a stone fence running through an old stand of trees, indicating that early settlers once cleared the land on one or both sides.

The lumber we use today is from forests that have been logged off three and four times since the first cutting. Our lumber is frequently full of knots and contains many more defects than the original trees. In New Hampshire it is not uncommon to find a beautiful stone fence running through an old stand of trees, indicating that the land had at one time been cleared for pasture on one or both sides of the fence.

All pieces in those days were built to serve a particular function—design was not an important concern. Unlike today's trends in furniture, the idea that "form follows function" surely applied. Some early pieces were actually out of proportion and somewhat awkward, but their character is obvious. This book has many projects with a lot of character!

Furniture and accessories made during the British rule were called "colonial," and those made after our independence from England are referred to as "early American." These designs did not change overnight, but there was a gradual evolution from colonial to early American style.

In doing the research for this book, I thought each and every project would be quite different, but after measuring, drawing, and building them all, I found to my surprise that they are very much alike in size and type of construction. Except for superficial outer design shapes, they are assembled much the same way, are very close to the same overall sizes, and serve the same functions regardless of their geographical origin, be it northern New Hampshire or southern Rhode Island.

Because each piece had a particular purpose, a purpose probably obsolete today, you must be imaginative in finding a use for each piece without destroying the design. Today an early pipe box, once used to store long-stemmed clay pipes and tobacco, can be used as a convenient place to store candles and matches, or for outgoing mail with stamps stored in the drawer; the many wall boxes in this book make great planters. Whatever their contemporary use, the projects reflect the independent spirit of those who lived in the early days of our country—a spirit passed on today to those who follow them in making these pieces.

Selecting Materials

As lumber for these projects will probably be the most expensive material you will purchase, it is a good idea to know a little about your choices. All lumber is either hardwood or softwood. Hardwoods are deciduous, trees that lose their leaves in the fall, and softwoods are coniferous, or evergreen. A few hardwoods are softer than some softwoods, but on the whole, hardwoods are stronger and much more durable. Tougher to work, hardwood takes a finish and a stain beautifully. It usually costs more than softwood but is well worth the difference in price.

All wood contains pores, or open spaces. Wood like oak and mahogany has pores that are very noticeable and should probably be filled for a nice appearance. Wood like maple and birch has what is called a "closed grain" and lends itself to a beautiful, smooth finish.

The grain of the wood is formed by the pattern of growth of that particular tree. Each year the circumference of a tree is girdled with an annular ring, which forms a new and hard fibrous layer. The growth of most trees is regular and these annular rings are evenly spaced, but in other trees the growth is very uneven, creating irregular spacing and thickness. The pattern formed by the rings is the grain pattern we see when the tree is cut into lumber.

The softwoods used for most of the projects in this book are pine, spruce, and fir. Pine was the favorite wood for colonial settlers because it was the easiest to work, especially for simple accessories like those found in this book. Hardwoods most used were maple, walnut, oak, cherry, poplar, and birch.

Always buy dried lumber. Green lumber will shrink, twist, and warp while drying. Purchase the best lumber you can find for these projects: Your work will be much easier and the finished project much better. The cost difference between an inexpensive piece of wood and the best you can find will be very little, as none of these small projects require much material.

Lumber is sold by the "board foot." A board foot is a piece of wood that is 1 inch thick, 12 inches wide, and 12 inches long. The formula, *in inches:*

width × thickness × length ÷ 144 = board feet

So a piece of wood 4 inches wide, 2 inches thick, and 6 feet (72 inches) long contains 4 board feet of lumber:

4 × 2 × 72 = 576
576 ÷ 144 = 4 board feet

For a quick, easy method to calculate board feet, see Figure 1. Given a particular thickness and width, find the corresponding "factor" and multiply it by the length of the board *in feet.* So a board 1 inch thick, 5 inches wide, and 12 feet long contains 5.004 board feet of lumber:

12 × 0.417 = 5.004

FIGURE I BOARD FEET

To calculate the number of board feet in a piece of lumber, locate the correct factor for the lumber's width and thickness, then multiply that factor by the lumber's lineal length (in feet).

WIDTH (INCHES)	THICKNESS	
	½ INCH	I INCH
2	.093	.167
3	.125	.250
4	.166	.333
5	.309	.417
6	.250	.500
8	.333	.666
10	.417	.833
12	.500	1.000

The term *lineal length* refers to the actual length of any board; dressed, or finished, lumber is smaller than its listed measurements because of the finishing process (see Figure 2).

A few projects call for wide boards, the best choice for authenticity. If you can't find them, glue narrow boards together to obtain the required width. Care should be given to matching grain patterns so that the joint will not be noticeable. Don't be concerned about strength, as a glued joint is as strong as a single piece of wood and probably will not warp.

Special hardwoods can be purchased from the mail-order suppliers listed at the end of this book. Some suppliers will cut and plane to exact size for the bill of materials list. Write or call them for details.

FIGURE 2

ROUGH LUMBER IN INCHES	FINISHED LUMBER IN INCHES
1 × 2	$3/4 \times 1^5/8$
1 × 3	$3/4 \times 2^5/8$
1 × 4	$3/4 \times 3^5/8$
1 × 5	$3/4 \times 4^5/8$
1 × 6	$3/4 \times 5^5/8$
1 × 8	$3/4 \times 7^1/2$
1 × 10	$3/4 \times 9^1/2$
1 × 12	$3/4 \times 11^1/2$

Making the Projects

After studying the plans, start by carefully making each part. Take care to make the pieces exactly to the correct size and square (90 degrees) to one another. Sand each piece separately, taking care to keep all edges sharp—some will be rounded after assembly.

     After all pieces have been made, dry fit them: that is, carefully put the project together to check for fit before final assembly. If anything needs refitting or is a poor fit, this is the time to correct it.

     If the pieces all fit correctly, glue or nail the project together, again taking care that all fits are tight and square. If you are using hardwood, drill holes just smaller than the nail diameter to avoid splitting the wood when nailing.

     Sand the project all over. It is at this time that the edges can be rounded if necessary, after which the project is ready for finishing.

IRREGULAR SHAPES

Many pieces featured here have curved or irregular shapes, which are illustrated on a grid. To draw these shapes full size, draw a grid on a sheet of paper or cardboard in the exact size indicated and carefully transfer the lines or points, square for square (see Figure 3).

     If you use paper, transfer the shape to the wood with a piece of carbon paper. If cardboard is used, cut out the pattern and transfer it directly to the wood. If the pattern is symmetrical—that is, the same on each side of the center—simply draw and transfer half the pattern to the wood at a time—this will ensure that the design will be perfect on both sides of the center.

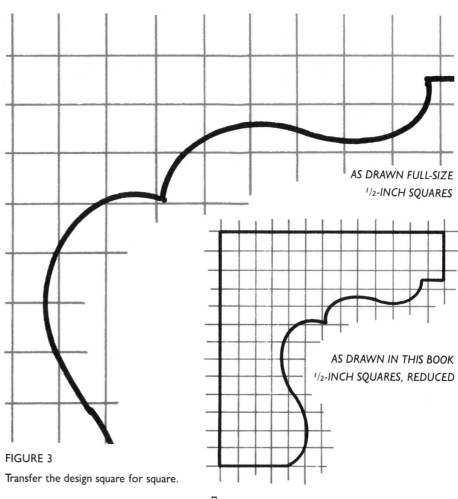

AS DRAWN FULL-SIZE
¹/₂-INCH SQUARES

AS DRAWN IN THIS BOOK
¹/₂-INCH SQUARES, REDUCED

FIGURE 3
Transfer the design square for square.

JOINTS

These projects use only four of the many kinds of joints available: the *butt joint*, the *rabbet joint*, the *dado joint*, and the *dovetail joint* (see Figure 4). They can be made by hand, without power tools, although the power tools will make the job easier.

Most projects in this book use the butt joint, the simplest of all joints. As its name implies, it is two boards that are butted up against each other and nailed together. The major disadvantage of the butt joint is that less wood is exposed for gluing or nailing. Also, nails sometimes back out of the joint over time, leaving an opening.

A rabbet joint is an L-shaped cut made along the edge of one board and overlapping the end of the other board. This joint is also nailed together, but the nails are hidden somewhat because they are put in from the sides. The front board of a drawer is a good example of a rabbet joint.

Dado joints are similar to rabbet joints except the cut leaves wood on both sides (see Figure 5). A drawer side is an excellent example of both a dado joint and a rabbet joint.

Dovetail joints were used on the sides of chests and drawers and on the tops of bureaus—they make a very tight joint and were usually used on better or more formal accessories (see Figure 6). Dovetailing was used in America starting around 1675. Early drawers used a dovetail joint for the front board and a dado joint for the back board, with one single, wide dovetail that was nailed in place. By 1730 drawers were made using three or four dovetails, and by 1800 and beyond dovetails had become very thin (see Figure 7).

FIGURE 4

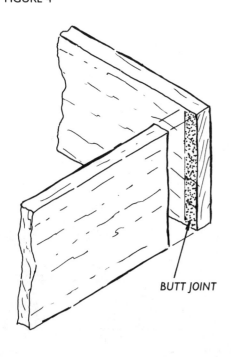

BUTT JOINT

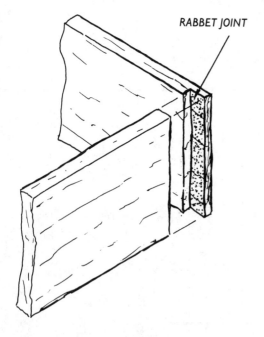

RABBET JOINT

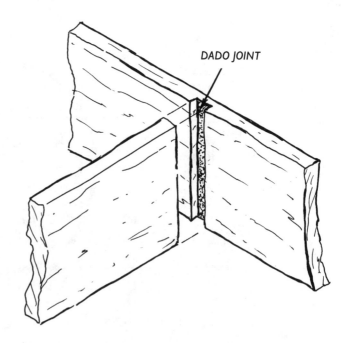

DADO JOINT

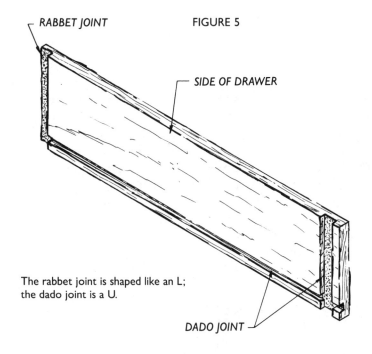

RABBET JOINT

FIGURE 5

SIDE OF DRAWER

DADO JOINT

The rabbet joint is shaped like an L;
the dado joint is a U.

FIGURE 6

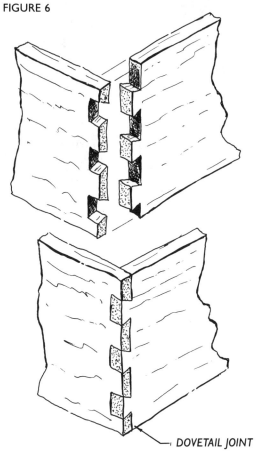

DOVETAIL JOINT

Dovetail joints are strong and tight . . . and not
as difficult to make as you might think.

FIGURE 7

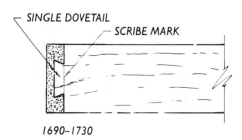

SINGLE DOVETAIL

SCRIBE MARK

1690–1730

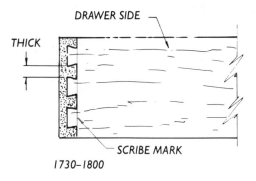

DRAWER SIDE

THICK

SCRIBE MARK

1730–1800

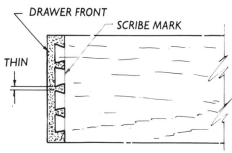

DRAWER FRONT

SCRIBE MARK

THIN

1800–1850

You can often tell the age of furniture from the
character of dovetail joints.

SHAPING

A few of the projects use molded edges or surfaces. These molded edges were probably done by hand with a special molding plane, a very satisfying method if you have the plane or can borrow one. Most of us do not have one at our disposal, however, so molded edges must be achieved by some other method. A scraper blade can be made by grinding a reverse profile into a piece of 1/16-inch-thick steel (see Figure 8) and used by scraping it into the wood, but perhaps the easiest method is to use a hand-held router. It is not very expensive and can make all the special edges required for the projects in this book.

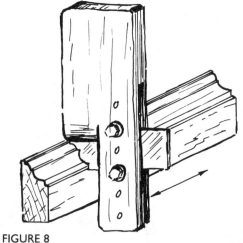

FIGURE 8
This handmade scraper blade will produce molded edges.

Crafters used this beader to create a decorative edge.

The router, perhaps the only power tool necessary for the projects in this book, can be used to make special edges. *(Courtesy of the Porter-Cable Corporation.)*

WORMHOLES

Some old pieces of furniture and accessories were attacked by insects that made what we call wormholes. The worms especially liked maple, walnut, oak, and most fruitwood, as well as pine and poplar. Wormholes appeared on the surface of the wood as small dots about the size of a pinhead. These holes can be faked using an ice pick or similar object.

A more obvious way to achieve wormholes is to use wood that has already been attacked by worms. (Wood with wormholes should be a good buy at the local lumberyard.) Because worms meander through wood, leaving channels going in all directions, wormy wood that has been sawed, planed or turned will show the side section of the wormholes, not the end or entrance. This is not authentic, but it does add that very old effect.

SCRIBE MARKS

Crafters of yesterday did not have pencils to mark off their work as we do today. Instead they used tools with sharp points to actually scratch, or "scribe," shallow grooves into the wood. These scribe marks can be seen on genuine antiques around dovetails, mortise joints, and in some cases, chair legs. To achieve that authentic look, you should consider using an awl or similar tool in place of a pencil to mark off your work. Leave the scribe marks on your finished project—they will add a lot to it and will indicate that it was handmade (see Figure 7).

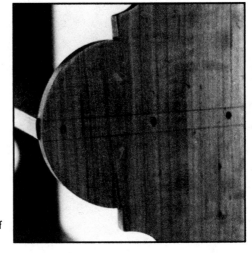

Early crafters used sharp, pointed tools instead of pencils to mark off, or "scribe," their work.

GLUING

Glue was not in general use until after 1750, so many of the originals of the projects featured in this book were simply nailed or pinned together. If, by chance, any were glued, they were probably joined with "hot" animal hide glue. Because very good glue is available today, it is advisable that your reproductions be glued as well as nailed.

Wood glues are either hot or cold, depending on whether heat is used to prepare them. Hot glue, made from animal parts, is very strong and quick setting. Until just a few years ago, hot glue was considered the only truly satisfactory kind of glue to use in cabinetmaking. Recent developments in new and better cold glues have made such generalizations debatable. Cold glues are synthetics and vary in durability and strength. Some are slow in setting, others fast. For the projects in this book cold yellow glue is recommended. In using cold glue, follow instructions given on the label.

Always take care to clean excess glue from around the joint. If you wait five to ten minutes, just until the glue is almost set, you can remove most of it with a chisel. Do not use a wet cloth; it will weaken the glue in the joint and the water will close the grain of the wood, making it harder to stain. For the few projects that are a little difficult to hold together while gluing, there is a new hot glue made not from animal hides but of glue sticks that are inserted into a glue gun, heated, and then pushed through the tip. This glue dries very quickly and sets in about ten seconds without clamping.

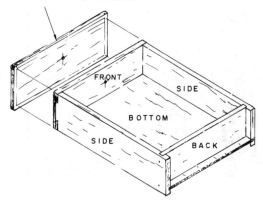

FIGURE 9

OVERLAPPING FRONT

A drawer is just a box without a top. The overlapping front is simply glued in place.

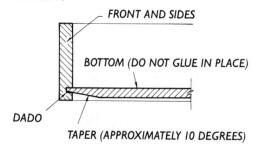

FIGURE 10

FRONT AND SIDES

BOTTOM (DO NOT GLUE IN PLACE)

DADO

TAPER (APPROXIMATELY 10 DEGREES)

The tapered edges of the bottom fit into the dado cuts of the front and sides.

DRAWER CONSTRUCTION

The drawer is easy to make. Think of it as a box without a top. Almost all drawers are made basically the same way, with a front, two sides, a bottom, and a back. All but two projects in this book use a simple kind of drawer that is called a "flush" drawer, which fits perfectly into the opening. The front piece does not overhang. Two or three projects use a drawer that has an overlapping drawer front. Both are easy to make, but the latter hides any imperfections in drawer construction or errors in size (see Figure 9).

To determine the size of the drawer, carefully measure the opening into which the drawer will fit. Record the height, width, and depth of the opening. Make the drawer about 1/32 to 1/16 inch less than the recorded height and about 1/16 to 3/32 inch less than the recorded width. The depth of the drawer should be about 1/16 inch shorter than the recorded depth.

Choose the wood for the drawer front carefully, as it should match the rest of the project. Try to find a piece of wood with an interesting grain pattern. The front piece should be thicker than the sides, back, and bottom, which are made of much thinner material and of secondary wood, such as pine or poplar.

Old drawer bottoms were usually chamfered (beveled) and set into grooves in the side and front boards of the drawer (see Figure 10). Do not glue the bottom board in place: Use two small nails, driven up from below and near the center of the bottom board.

As the drawer for each project will be slightly different, study Figures 11 and 12 before starting construction. Remember, original bottom boards had tapered sides.

Many drawers made after 1720 had handmade dovetail joints. These joints look difficult to make but are actually fairly easy and fun to do. There are many excellent books and magazines that illustrate how to make a dovetail joint.

FIGURE 11

TWO SMALL NAILS

For authenticity, do not use glue. Instead, secure the bottom by driving two small nails through the bottom into the back. Shown is a flush drawer.

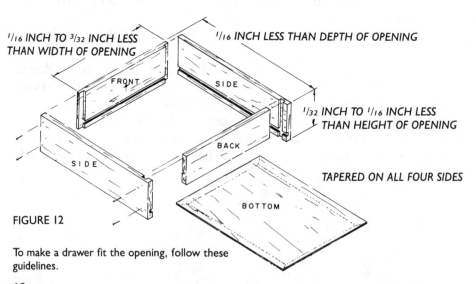

1/16 INCH TO 3/32 INCH LESS THAN WIDTH OF OPENING

1/16 INCH LESS THAN DEPTH OF OPENING

1/32 INCH TO 1/16 INCH LESS THAN HEIGHT OF OPENING

TAPERED ON ALL FOUR SIDES

FIGURE 12

To make a drawer fit the opening, follow these guidelines.

Hardware

As with lumber, the extra money spent on high-quality, authentic hardware adds little to the overall cost of the project and is well worth the difference. At the end of this book is a list of quality vendors that sell such hardware; flea markets are another good place to look. An old, authentic hinge, though rusty and worn, will add a lot of character to your project and will really make it look original.

PINS

Because nails were so expensive, wooden pins were sometimes used in their place, especially in mortise and tenon joints. Early pins were referred to as "trunnels." Some were tapered, but contrary to popular belief, none were round in cross section. Rather they were polygonal or even square, made that way so that the edges of the pin would bite into the round hole into which they were driven, securing them tightly. If you use pins on any projects in this book, take care not to use round, dowel-like pins. Leave the ends projecting from the surface 1/16 inch or more to simulate old age, and drill the holes for the pins at a slight angle to improve holding power (see Figure 13).

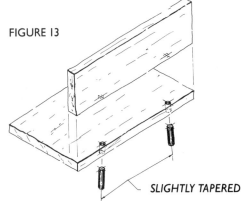

FIGURE 13

SLIGHTLY TAPERED

Tapered pins, or trunnels, that are driven in at a slight angle will hold tightly.

NAILS

Nails were used to hold parts of early country accessories in place. Glue would not have been used on such simple objects as those found in this book. From the seventeenth century probably through to the nineteenth century, nails were hand forged from pure iron. They were rust-resistant and bent very easily but seldom broke. Early hand-forged nails were square in cross section and tapered on all four sides to a point (see Figure 14). Hand-forged nails range in size from tiny brads, used to apply moldings, to large common nails, used for construction of buildings and bridges. Early nails had bumpy "rose" heads, square heads, or sometimes no heads at all. Because they were hand forged, one at a time, no two nails were made exactly alike.

Machine-cut square nails, somewhat resembling original hand-forged nails, were made from 1790 to 1870 or so. They are rectangular in cross section and tapered on two opposite sides (see Figure 14). Machine-cut nails made in large quantities after 1815 had blunt, squared-off points and tended to rust.

Today, machine-cut nails can be purchased from several suppliers for very reasonable prices; see the list at the back of this book. It is recommended that these nails be used in building the projects to give your work an authentic look and feel, but you can safely use "modern" (c. 1870) roundhead steel wire nails as well. After the project is completed, they will not be seen—only you will know.

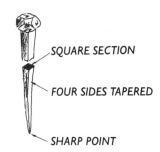

FIGURE 14

SQUARE SECTION

FOUR SIDES TAPERED

SHARP POINT

HANDMADE NAIL

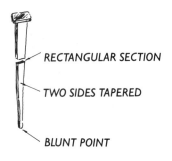

RECTANGULAR SECTION

TWO SIDES TAPERED

BLUNT POINT

MACHINE-MADE NAIL

FIGURE 15

HANDMADE SCREW

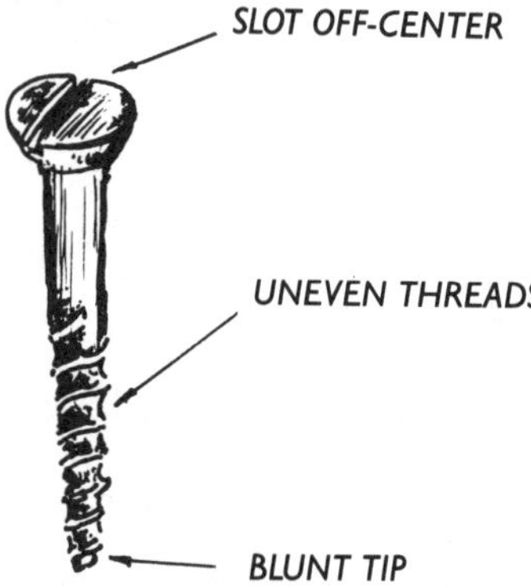

SLOT OFF-CENTER

UNEVEN THREADS

BLUNT TIP

SCREWS

Screws were used as early as 1700. Like nails, the first screws were made by hand but were much more expensive to produce than nails, so they were not used nearly as much—especially in primitive or early country accessories, such as those in this book.

Early screws were only $1/2$ inch in length or shorter. Their threads were made by hand and were uneven, wide, and rounded on the edges. The tips of the threads were blunt, and the heads flat. The slot was narrow, shallow, and often off center. See Figure 15.

Machine-cut screws were invented around 1815. The first screws were somewhat like the handmade screws but tended to be longer. By 1850 machine-cut screws were exactly like those of today.

FIGURE 16

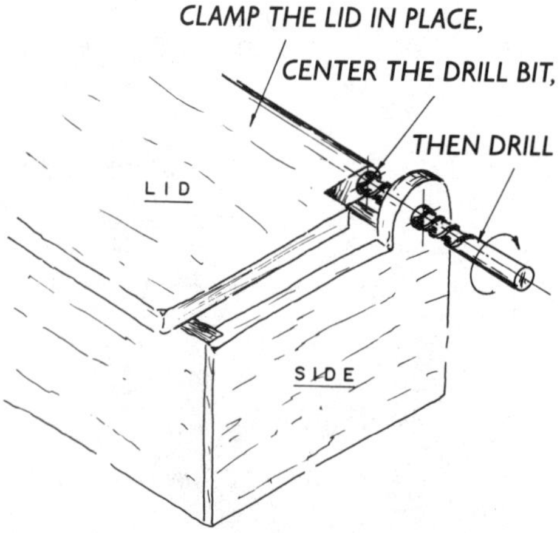

CLAMP THE LID IN PLACE,

CENTER THE DRILL BIT,

THEN DRILL

LID

SIDE

Drilling the hole for the dowel with the lid in place will give a good fit.

HINGES

Wood dowel hinge

Four projects in this book use wooden hinges to support the lids. A wood dowel hinge is made by extending the sides of the box above the lid, drilling a hole through the sides into the lid, and inserting two wood dowels (or nails) through the holes (see Figure 16). These hinges are simple to make and give the impression of being very old. Take care, however, to drill the hole into the lid after the holes in the sides have been drilled. A good way of ensuring a perfect fit is to clamp or secure the lid in place, exactly as it is to be when closed, and drill the holes into the lid through the holes in the side pieces, as illustrated. Add the wood dowels last.

FIGURE 17

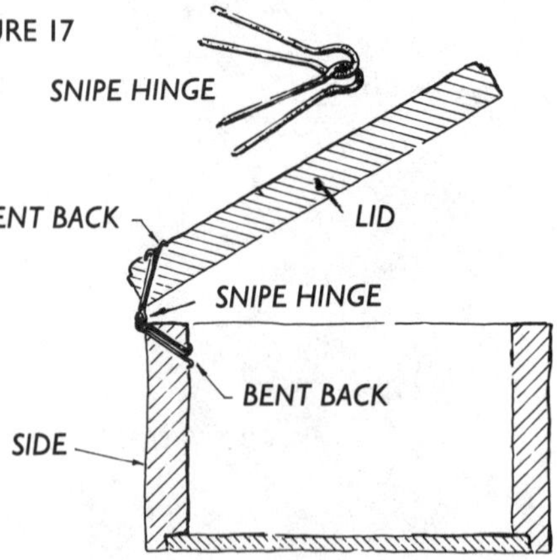

SNIPE HINGE

BENT BACK

LID

SNIPE HINGE

BENT BACK

SIDE

This section view of a lidded box shows how a snipe hinge works. Bend the points back and drive them into the wood.

Snipe hinge

Another old type of hinge is the "snipe" hinge, sometimes referred to as a staple hinge, clinch hinge, or cotterpin hinge. One of the earliest hinges, it is like two hairpins joined together (see Figure 17).

Snipe hinges were hand forged from two iron rods that ranged from $1/16$ inch to $3/32$ inch thick with pointed ends. The sharp pointed ends were inserted into holes in furniture at an angle, with the points poking through the other side (see Figure 17). The protruding points were spread apart and "clinched," or bent back around and driven into the other side of the wood. These hinges wore out very quickly. It is not uncommon to find early pieces that have modern hinges alongside the original snipe hinges.

Snipe hinges were used mostly on chest lids and sometimes on cupboard doors from 1719 to 1800.

Butterfly hinge

These hinges were used from 1700 to around 1765. They were called butterfly hinges because of their splayed sides (see Figure 18). Hand-forged hinges were thicker through the center section and thinner at the edges. They were attached with handmade screws or rosehead nails. The nails were usually clinched back through the wood from behind.

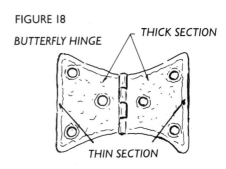

FIGURE 18
BUTTERFLY HINGE
THICK SECTION
THIN SECTION

Butt hinge

Butt hinges, easily identified by their square ends, were used as early as 1815 (see Figure 19). They are usually set into shallow mortises in the wood, so the hinge is flush with the surface (see Figure 20).

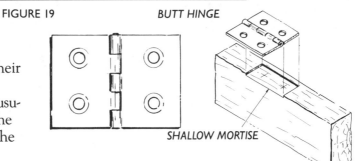

FIGURE 19

BUTT HINGE

SHALLOW MORTISE

FIGURE 20

The butt hinge usually sits flush with the surface of the wood.

KNOBS

Wooden knobs, originally referred to as "thumb-pulls," were probably the first kind of knob used on early American country accessories and furniture. They were almost always made of hardwood and were sometimes of a different wood than the piece itself.

A few projects in this book call for metal knobs. Usually brass, these tended to be more formal in design than wooden knobs. Brass knobs made their appearance in America around 1675 and were cast brass.

Original brass knobs were meant to be highly polished. Through the years, however, people came to believe that old brasses should be left tarnished. Today many inexpensive reproductions are made to look tarnished, which is incorrect. Original polished brass was also very light in color. It was not until after 1755 that more copper was added to the brass, which tended to make it darker, as it is today.

Original wooden knobs were generally longer than they were wide and ranged from 1 inch to 2 inches in length (see Figure 21). Some knobs were driven into a hole of a smaller diameter than the knob shank (see Figure 22). Others were held in place by a wooden peg driven through a small hole in the shank (see Figure 23), which is what is used for most of the projects in this book. Sometime after 1825, as screws became more available, hardwood knobs were held in place by screws inserted from behind (see Figure 24).

Later, wooden knobs tended to be wider than they were long. Called mushroom knobs, they were fastened using the same methods as the early knobs. Figure 25 offers some designs to copy if you have a lathe.

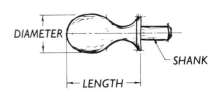

FIGURE 21

DIAMETER
SHANK
LENGTH

Early knobs were usually longer than their diameters.

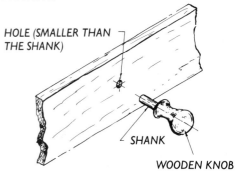

FIGURE 22

HOLE (SMALLER THAN THE SHANK)

SHANK

WOODEN KNOB

So that a wooden knob fits tightly, drill the hole slightly smaller than the diameter of the shank.

FIGURE 23

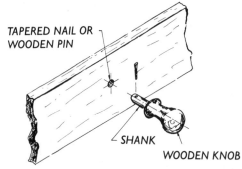

TAPERED NAIL OR WOODEN PIN

SHANK

WOODEN KNOB

To attach a wooden knob with a pin, drill a hole in the shank x inches along the shank, where x equals the thickness of the drawer front plus half the diameter of the pin.

"x"

If you are going to use modern purchased knobs, you can make them look older by drilling a hole into each and gluing a dowel into the hole (see Figure 26).

FIGURE 25

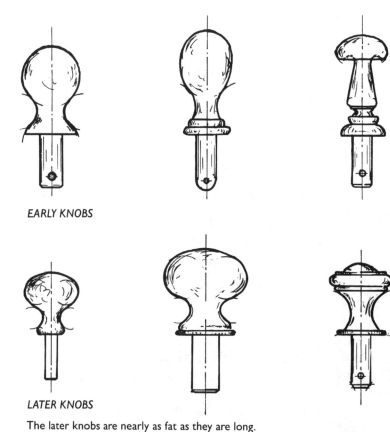

EARLY KNOBS

LATER KNOBS

The later knobs are nearly as fat as they are long.

FIGURE 24

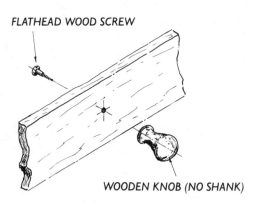

FLATHEAD WOOD SCREW

WOODEN KNOB (NO SHANK)

This hardwood knob is attached to the drawer with a screw.

FIGURE 26

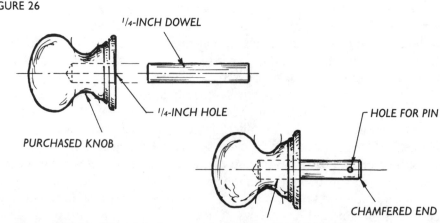

¹/₄-INCH DOWEL

¹/₄-INCH HOLE

PURCHASED KNOB

HOLE FOR PIN

CHAMFERED END

DOWEL, GLUED IN PLACE

To make a modern wooden knob look more authentic, drill a hole and glue a dowel in place, as a substitute for a shank. Secure the knob to the drawer front with a tapered nail or wooden pin.

Finishing and Staining

After completing construction, you will be ready to finish your project. This is the important part and should not be rushed. Remember, the finish will be seen for years to come. No matter how good the wood and hardware and no matter how tight the joints, a poor finish will ruin your project.

PREPARING

Step 1. All joints should be checked for tight fits. If necessary, apply water putty to them and allow ample time for them to dry. For the projects found in this book it will probably not be necessary to set and fill nailheads; they are generally left showing. If you do not want to see the nailheads, however, set and water-putty them now.

Step 2. Sand the project all over in the direction of the grain. If sanding is done by hand, use a sanding block and keep all corners sharp until Step 3. Use an 80-grit paper first, then resand all over using a 120-grit paper and, if necessary, again using a 180-grit paper.

Step 3. If you want any of the edges slightly rounded, now is the time to do so. First, carefully study the object and try to imagine how it would have been used through the years. Then, using a rasp, judiciously round the edges where you think wear would have occurred. Finally, sand the entire project and the new "worn" edges with 120-grit paper, then with 180-grit paper.

Step 4. Distressing will help make these copies of 150-year-old antiques look old. It can be done many ways. Roll a piece of coral stone about 3 inches in diameter, or a similar object, across the various surfaces. Don't be afraid to add a few scratches at random here and there, especially on the bottoms or backs, where an object would have been worn the most.

Step 5. Carefully check that all surfaces are smooth, dry, and dust-free, especially if softwood is used.

A palm grip sander is useful in completing these projects, but they can also be sanded by hand. *(Courtesy of the Porter-Cable Corporation.)*

A 3-inch coral stone or similar object is rolled across the surface of the wood for distress marks, which help make the piece look old.

FILLERS

A paste filler should be used for porous wood, such as oak or mahogany. Purchase paste filler slightly darker than the color of your wood, which will turn darker with age. Before using paste filler, thin it with turpentine so that it can be brushed on. Use a stiff brush and brush with the grain to fill the pores. In fifteen or twenty minutes, wipe off the filler across the grain with a piece of burlap, taking care to leave filler in the pores. Apply a second coat if necessary and let dry for twenty-four hours.

STAINING

The two major kinds of stain are water stain and oil stain. Water stains are purchased in powder form and mixed as needed by dissolving the powder in hot water. They have a tendency to raise the grain of the wood. If a water stain is used, the surface should be lightly sanded with fine paper after it dries. Oil stains are made from pigments ground in linseed oil; they do not raise the grain. You'll want to follow the instructions given on the container, whichever kind of stain you use, but here is the basic procedure.

Step 1. Test the stain on a scrap piece of the lumber you're using to make certain it will be the color you want.

Step 2. Wipe or brush on the stain as quickly and as evenly as possible to avoid overlapping streaks. If a darker finish is desired, apply more than one coat of stain. Try not to apply too much stain on the end grain, as it will darken much more. Allow the piece to dry in a dust-free area for at least twenty-four hours.

FINISHES

Shellac provides a hard surface, is easy to apply, and dries in a few hours. For best results, thin slightly with alcohol and apply three or four light coats. Several coats of thin shellac are much better than one or two thick coats. Sand lightly with extra-fine paper between coats, but be sure afterward to rub the entire surface with a dampened cloth to remove any dust. For that antique effect, strive for a smooth, satin finish, not a high-gloss coat.

Varnish is easy to brush on and dries to a smooth, hard finish within twenty-four hours. It makes an excellent transparent, deep-looking finish. Be sure to apply varnish in a completely dust-free area. Apply one or two coats directly from the can with long even strokes. Rub with 0000 steel wool between each coat and after the last coat. As with shellac, do not leave a glossy finish—an antique would not have a high gloss after 150 years.

Oil finishes are especially easy to use for projects like those in this book. They are easy to apply, long lasting, and improve wood permanently, and they never need resanding. Apply a heavy, wet coat uniformly to all surfaces and let it set for twenty or thirty minutes. Wipe dry or until you have a nice satin finish.

WASH COAT

Even with the distress marks and scratches, your project probably still looks new. To give your project a 150-year-old look, take a cloth and simply wipe on a coat of oil-base black paint directly from the can. Take care to get the black paint in all distress marks and scratches. Wipe off all paint immediately, before it dries, but leave the black paint in all the corners, joints, scratches, and distress marks. If you goof or don't like your work, simply wipe the paint off with turpentine on a cloth. This wash coat should make your project look like an original antique.

FOR THE LOOK OF OLD PAINT

Follow the first five steps outlined for preparing your project for finishing.

Step 6. Seal the wood with a light coat of 50 percent alcohol and 50 percent shellac. After it is dry, rub lightly with 0000 steel wool and wipe clean.

Step 7. Apply an even coat of paint, taking care to use an old color (see the suppliers' list at the end of the book for recommended paints). Let dry for forty-eight hours. Do not paint the backs or bottoms—in the originals, these parts were seldom painted.

Step 8. With 120-grit paper, sand all the rounded edges you made for "wear" marks in Step 4. If these edges were worn, the paint surely would have worn off also. Sand away paint from all sharp edges and corners; they, too, would wear through the years.

Step 9. Lightly sand all over with 180-grit paper to remove new paint gloss. Wipe clean.

Step 10. With a cloth, wipe on a coat of oil-base black paint directly from the can. Take care to get the black paint in all corners, distress marks, and scratches. Don't forget the unpainted back and bottom. Wipe the paint off immediately, before it dries, but leave it in all corners, joints, scratches, and distress marks. If you apply too much, wipe off with turpentine-dipped cloth. Let dry for twenty-four hours. Apply a light coat of paste wax.

FOR EXTRA AGING

For that extra-aged look, apply two coats of paint, each a different color, such as powder blue for the first coat and antique brick red for the second. Allow twenty-four hours between coats. After the second coat has dried for forty-eight hours or more, follow Steps 8 and 9, but sand through the top coat so that the first color shows through here and there at worn areas. Finish with Step 10. This technique is especially good on such projects as footstools or large painted wall boxes.

Extra aging can be simulated by applying two coats of paint, each a different color, and sanding the top coat at the worn areas so that the first color shows through.

FOR A CRINKLE FINISH

If you wish to give your painted project an aged, crinkle finish, follow these steps. After Step 6 in preparing your project, apply a coat of liquid hide glue over the surfaces to be painted. Let dry for twelve hours and then paint a coat of gesso over the glue. Paint lightly, and do not go over any strokes. In ten to fifteen seconds the gesso will start to crinkle. Let dry for twenty-four hours in a very dry area. After twenty-four hours or more, continue to Steps 7 through 10. (Experiment on scrap wood first.)

Visits to museums, antique shops, and flea markets will provide you with a realistic idea of what an antique should look like and what kind of finish will make your reproduction look 150 years old.

By achieving such a look, you will produce a project that appears to be authentic, and you may have fun fooling your friends into thinking it's an antique. If you sell the piece, avoid legal problems by making certain that potential buyers know it is a reproduction only.

SMOKE GRAINING

Smoke graining was a very crude process common folk used on pine to simulate the expensive walnut and mahogany wood that only aristocrats could afford. (*Note:* You may want to practice this technique on a scrap of wood before attempting it on your project.)

Paint the piece whatever brown-base color you wish and let it dry twenty-four hours. Sand it smooth and apply a coat of varnish. Wait about two hours, or until the surface is tacky. Attach a *short*—2 inches or so—candle to a tuna fish can, which will catch the drippings.

If your project is small, hold the piece in one hand and move the candle underneath, using a sweeping motion. If the piece is large, however, you will have to hold it above the candle and, in effect, work upside down, also using the sweeping motion. Keep the piece 3 to 4 inches above the flame so that it doesn't blister.

For more smoke, hold a large nail or similar object in the flame, but be careful not to burn yourself in the process. Do not work in a draft.

Should you make a mistake during this process, let the varnish dry completely, then lightly sand the piece again, repaint with the base color, and start over. In the event that the varnish blisters, sand it down until it's smooth (don't strip off the base color), apply another coat of varnish, and when that coat is tacky, begin with the candle again.

After you achieve the desired effect, allow to dry for twenty-four hours. Taking care not to blur the smoking effect, apply a final coat of varnish using a bristle varnish brush (do not use a nylon brush).

Let dry twenty-four hours and sand lightly with a fine sandpaper. Wipe with a soft rag and add a coat of paste wax. Your reproduction is now ready for use for the next 150 years.

How to Use the Drawings

With each project there is a two-view drawing; one view is the *front view* and the other is either the *right view* or the *top view*. The views are positioned so that the front view is always the most important view and the starting place for studying the drawings. The right view is located directly to the right of the front view and the top view is located directly above the front view.

Dash lines indicate hidden surfaces or features within the object. Think of these lines as X rays showing what the inside will look like. Most drawer assemblies are shown with dash lines.

At times a *section view* is used to further illustrate a particular feature of the project. The section view is a partial view and illustrates only a portion of the project, such as a detail of a drawer construction

Each project also has an *exploded view*, which illustrates the project as it is to be put together. Study the drawings until you fully understand how the project is to be assembled before you begin work.

Each project includes a bill of materials list, occasionally called a cutting list. This list notes the exact size and quantity of material needed to make this project. Cut all pieces to exact size and sand all edges and surfaces before starting.

There are many dimensions in this book. Each has been checked and rechecked, but as you know, Murphy's Law can creep into anything, so it is a good idea for you to recheck all cuts as you proceed.

Individual parts are numbered in the order they should be assembled. Any purchased parts should be ordered before starting your project so that you can fit them to the project if necessary.

The Projects

Cutting Board

This is a copy of a cutting board I saw hanging in a restored house at Shelburne Museum in northern Vermont. It is simple to make, and it can be made with hardwood scraps. If you need to glue material together for the 9$\frac{1}{8}$-inch width, use a waterproof glue.

Step 1. Study the plans carefully. As you do so, visualize how you will make the cutting board and what tools you will need.

Step 2. Because this project has an irregular shape, it should be laid out on a ½-inch grid to make a full-size pattern. Transfer the shape of the piece to the grid. Draw the top section with a compass.

Step 3. Lightly sand all surfaces and edges with medium sandpaper to remove any burrs or tool marks. Keep all edges square and sharp.

Step 4. Finish to suit, using a nontoxic finish such as Salad Bowl or salad oil.

Step 5. Add a leather strap and your antique is ready to hang.

24

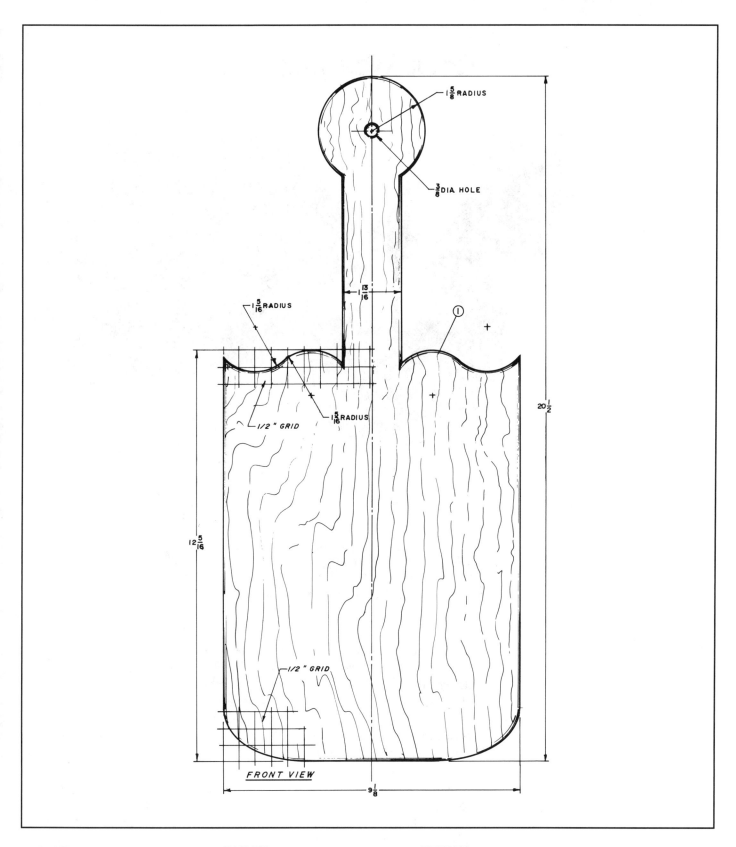

FRONT VIEW

$1\frac{5}{8}$ RADIUS

$\frac{3}{8}$ DIA HOLE

$1\frac{5}{16}$ RADIUS

$1\frac{5}{16}$ RADIUS

1/2" GRID

1/2" GRID

$1\frac{3}{16}$

$20\frac{1}{2}$

$12\frac{5}{16}$

$9\frac{1}{8}$

PART	INCHES	NEEDED
1 BOARD	$3/4 \times 9^{1}/_{8} \times 20^{1}/_{2}$	1

Cock Weather Vane

In Colonial America weather vane motifs were limited to a few basic designs, such as arrows, roosters, fish, Indians, and even grasshoppers. The designs usually reflected special or local interest; for example, early churches used Christian symbols, such as cocks, fish, and angels. Farmers used horses, cows, sheep, pigs, hens, and other livestock themes to adorn their houses and barns. Along the Atlantic coast, fish, whales, ships, and even serpents were popular.

Early weather vanes were carved from pine and painted white, Indian red, or yellow ochre. This early cock pattern can be painted or left to weather naturally.

Step 1. Study the plans carefully, checking the shape of each part. Visualize how you will make the weather vane and what tools you will need.

Step 2. Because this project has an irregular shape, it should be laid out on a ½-inch grid to make a full-size pattern. Transfer the shape of the weather vane to the grid.

Step 3. Lightly sand all surfaces and edges with medium sandpaper to remove any burrs or tool marks. Keep all edges square and sharp.

Step 4. Drill the ³/8-inch-diameter through the body.

Step 5. Make a stand ¾ inch thick by 4½ inches wide by 12 inches long. Drill a ³/8-inch-diameter hole in the center of the board.

Step 6. Cut a ³/8-inch-diameter dowel 10 to 12 inches long.

Step 7. The 1½-inch-diameter ball can be turned or purchased. Drill a ³/8-inch-diameter hole into the ball and mount it on the dowel.

Step 8. Assemble as shown.

Step 9. Finish to suit using the general finishing instructions. For a unique look, try a crinkle finish, burn the surface lightly with a torch, or use a wire brush. The original was painted brick red.

Pattern begins on next page.

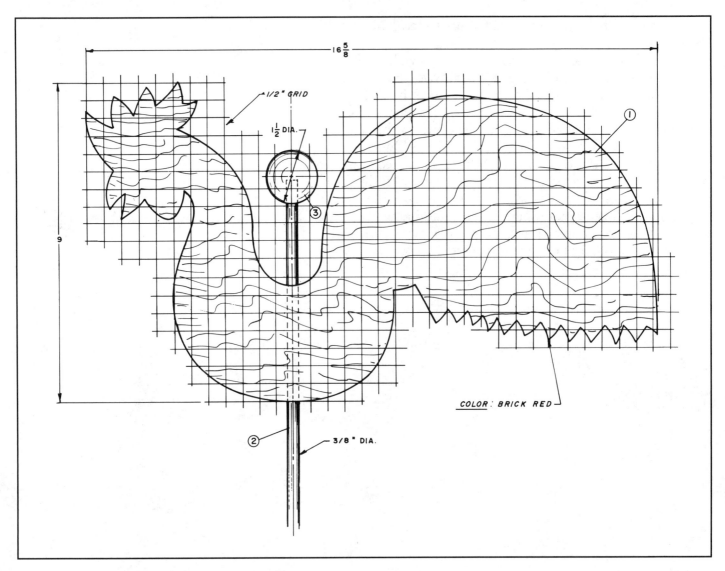

PART	INCHES	NEEDED
1 BODY	$\frac{3}{4} \times 9 \times 16\frac{5}{8}$	1
2 POST	$\frac{3}{8}$ DIA.	1
3 BALL	$1\frac{1}{2}$ DIA.	1

Simple Wall Shelf

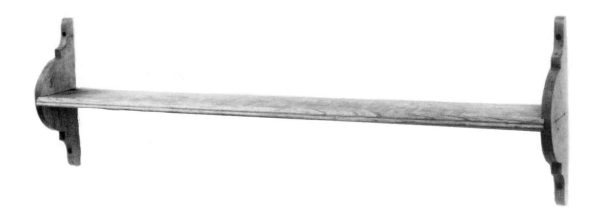

This little wall shelf, perfect for displaying miniatures, is patterned after a northern Vermont antique. Although the shelf pictured is 50 inches long, it can be made almost any length. It has an unusual ¼-inch bead along the front edge; however, if you don't have the tools to make a bead, make a straight plain edge. The shelf can be painted or stained to suit.

Step 1. Study the plans carefully, checking the shape of each part. Visualize how you will make the shelf and what tools you will need.

Step 2. As you study the plans, note the order in which the project is to be assembled.

Step 3. The irregular part should be laid out on a ½-inch grid to make a full-size pattern. Transfer the shape of the piece to the grid.

Step 4. Carefully cut all parts according to the materials list. Cut all parts to exact size and cut the edges exactly square (90°). Recheck all dimensions.

Step 5. Lightly sand all surfaces and edges with medium sandpaper to remove any burrs or tool marks. Keep all edges square and sharp.

Step 6. Follow the detailed illustrations and dimensions for making the parts. To make the ¼-inch bead, first cut the front edge of the board at 45° as shown. Use a router with an ⅛-inch radius to cut the bead. Depending on your bit, you may have to use a table saw and recut the notch just below the bead as shown. (Some bits might cut the notch as you cut the bead.)

Step 7. Check all dimensions for accuracy. Resand with fine-grit paper, keeping all edges sharp.

Step 8. After all the pieces have been made, dry-fit them; that is, assemble the complete project without glue or nails to check for accuracy and joint fit. If any parts fit poorly, now is the time to make corrections.

Step 9. Assemble the shelf, keeping everything square. Leave the square-cut nails showing.

Step 10. Finish to suit, using the general finishing instructions.

Pattern begins on next page.

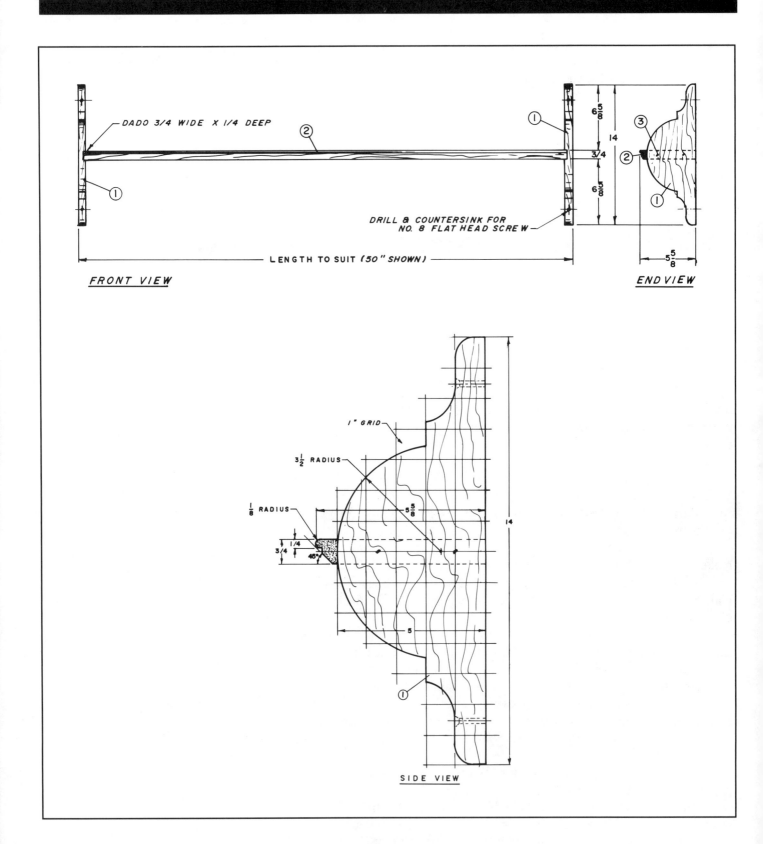

DADO 3/4 WIDE X 1/4 DEEP

② ①

DRILL & COUNTERSINK FOR
NO. 8 FLAT HEAD SCREW

LENGTH TO SUIT (50" SHOWN)

$6\frac{5}{8}$
14
$3/4$
$6\frac{5}{8}$

③ ②
①

$5\frac{5}{8}$

FRONT VIEW   _END VIEW_

1" GRID

$3\frac{1}{2}$ RADIUS

$\frac{1}{8}$ RADIUS

$5\frac{5}{8}$

14

1/4
3/4
45°

5

①

SIDE VIEW

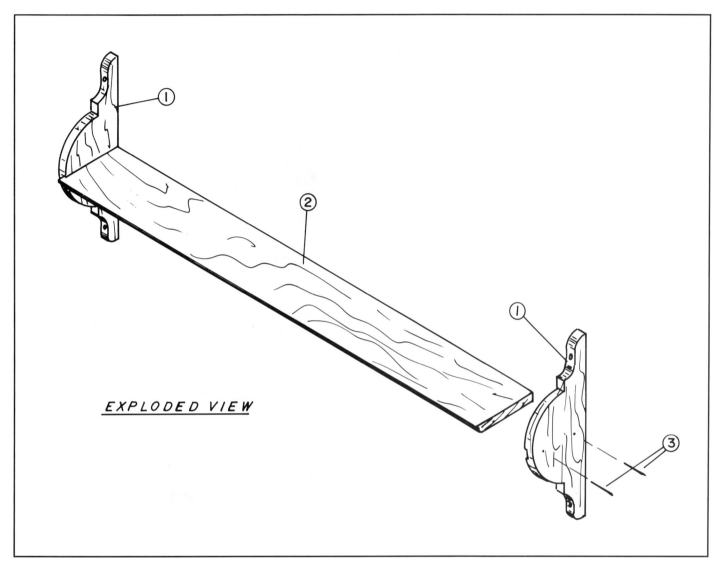

EXPLODED VIEW

PART	INCHES	NEEDED
1 END	$3/4 \times 5 \times 14$	2
2 SHELF	$3/4 \times 5^5/8 \times 50$	1
3 SQUARE-CUT FINISH NAIL	$1^1/2$ LONG	4

Small Wall Box

This unusual box is so small that I can't imagine what it was used for. This project can be stained to suit; I suggest a crinkle finish.

Step 1. Study the plans carefully, checking the shape of each part. Visualize how you will make the box and what tools you will need.

Step 2. As you study the plans, note the order in which the project is to be assembled.

Step 3. Because the back (part 1) has an irregular shape, it should be laid out on a ½-inch grid to make a full-size pattern. Transfer the shape of the piece to the grid.

Step 4. Carefully cut all parts according to the materials list. Cut all parts to exact size and cut the edges exactly square (90°). Recheck all dimensions.

Step 5. Lightly sand all surfaces and edges with medium sandpaper to remove any burrs or tool marks. Keep all edges square and sharp.

Step 6. Follow the detailed illustrations and dimensions for making the parts. Check all dimensions for accuracy. Resand with fine-grit paper, keeping all edges sharp.

Step 7. After all the pieces have been made, dry-fit them; that is, assemble the complete project without glue or nails to check for accuracy and joint fit. If any parts fit poorly, now is the time to make corrections.

Step 8. Assemble the box, keeping everything square. Leave the square-cut nails showing.

Step 9. Finish to suit, using the general finishing instructions.

Pattern begins on next page.

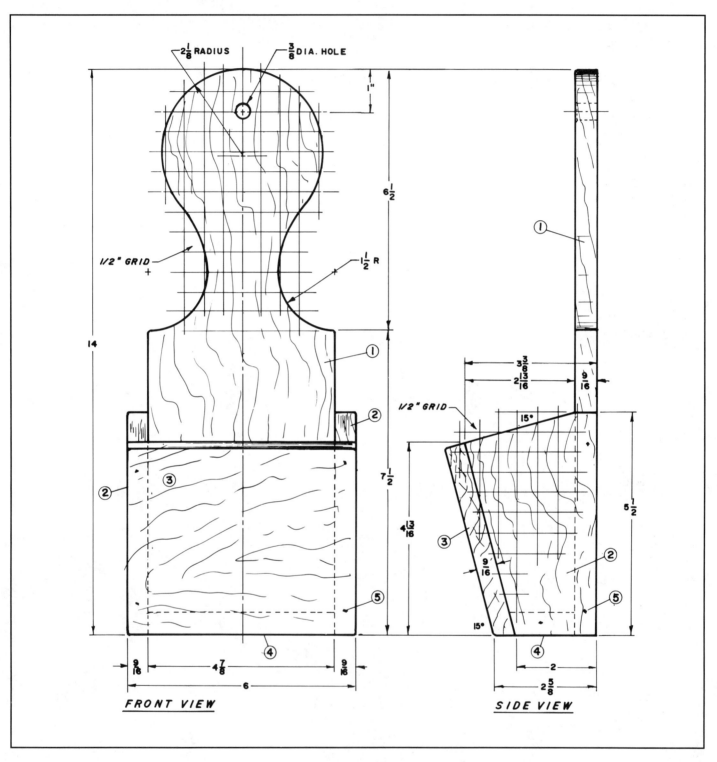

FRONT VIEW

SIDE VIEW

PART	INCHES	NEEDED
1 BACK	$^9/_{16} \times 4^7/_8 \times 14$	1
2 SIDE	$^9/_{16} \times 3^3/_8 \times 5^1/_2$	2
3 FRONT	$^9/_{16} \times 5 \times 6$	1
4 BOTTOM	$^9/_{16} \times 1^5/_8 \times 4^7/_8$	1
5 SQUARE-CUT FINISH NAIL	$1^1/_4$	10

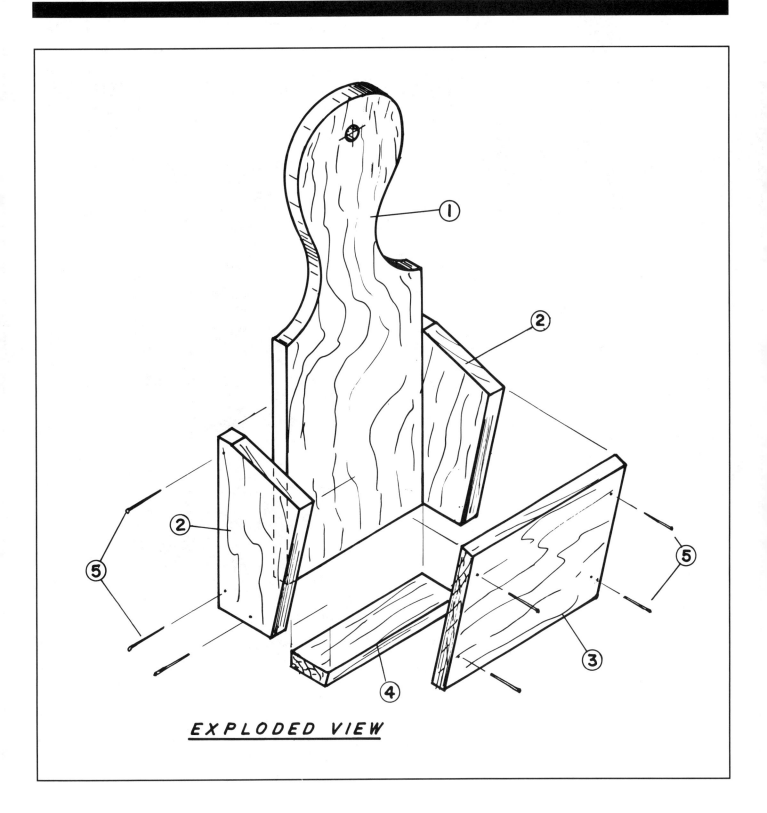

EXPLODED VIEW

Fishtail Wall Box with Drawer

In early America, fishing was a major industry along the coast, and many items that were used daily included a decorative fishtail motif. The fishtail design was common on weather vanes, signs, and furniture, as well as on Eli Terry's popular pillar and scroll clock. A hardwood, such as cherry, walnut, or maple, is recommended for this formal wall box and drawer.

Step 1. Study the plans carefully, checking the shape of each part. Visualize how you will make the fishtail wall box and its drawer and what tools you will need.

Step 2. As you study the plans, note the order in which the project is to be assembled.

Step 3. Because the back (part 1) has an irregular shape, it should be laid out on a ½-inch grid to make a full-size pattern. Transfer the shape of the piece to the grid.

Step 4. Carefully cut all parts according to the materials list. Cut all parts to exact size and cut the edges exactly square (90°). Recheck all dimensions.

Step 5. Lightly sand all surfaces and edges with medium sandpaper to remove any burrs or tool marks. Keep all edges square and sharp.

Step 6. Follow the detailed illustrations and dimensions for making the parts. Check all dimensions for accuracy. Resand with fine-grit paper, keeping all edges sharp.

Step 7. After all the pieces have been made, dry-fit them; that is, assemble the complete project without glue or nails to check for accuracy and joint fit. If any parts fit poorly, now is the time to make corrections.

Step 8. Turn or purchase the ⅝-inch-diameter knob (part 10). The knob does not need to be exactly perfect, so you could carve one. Many early knobs were handmade without a lathe. Pin the knob in place as illustrated; a small square-cut finish nail works well as a pin.

Step 9. Assemble the wall box, keeping everything square.

Step 10. Finish to suit, using the general finishing instructions. Do not paint this box. Instead, put a clear topcoat over the hardwood.

Pattern begins on next page.

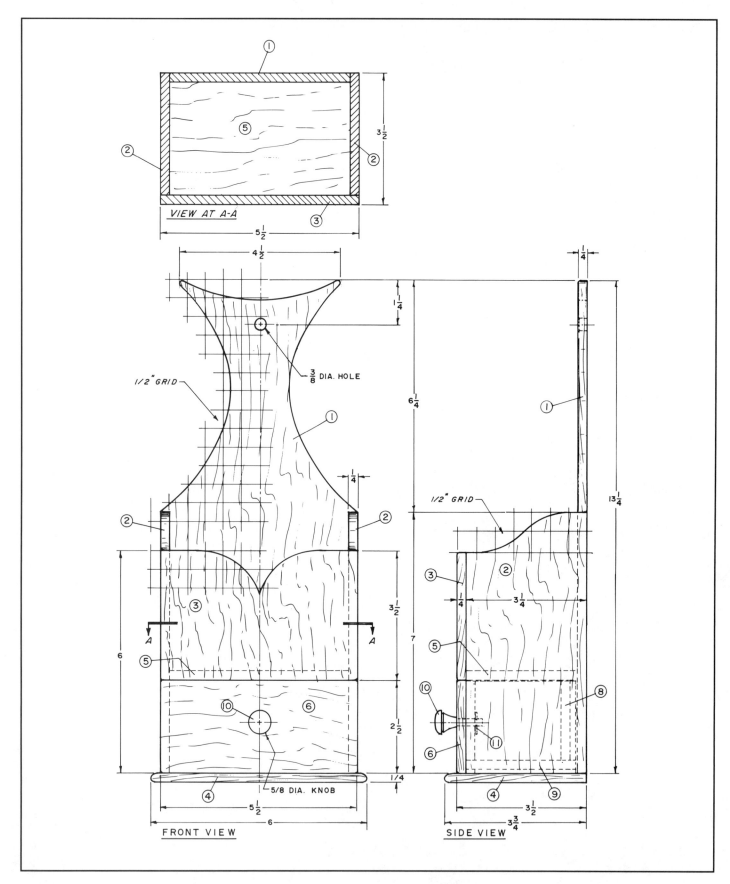

VIEW AT A-A

$3\frac{1}{2}$

$5\frac{1}{2}$

$4\frac{1}{2}$

$\frac{1}{4}$

$1\frac{1}{4}$

$\frac{3}{8}$ DIA. HOLE

1/2" GRID

$6\frac{1}{4}$

$13\frac{1}{4}$

1/2" GRID

$\frac{1}{4}$

$3\frac{1}{4}$

$3\frac{1}{2}$

A   A

6

7

$2\frac{1}{2}$

$\frac{1}{4}$

5/8 DIA. KNOB

$5\frac{1}{2}$

6

FRONT VIEW

$3\frac{1}{2}$

$3\frac{3}{4}$

SIDE VIEW

38

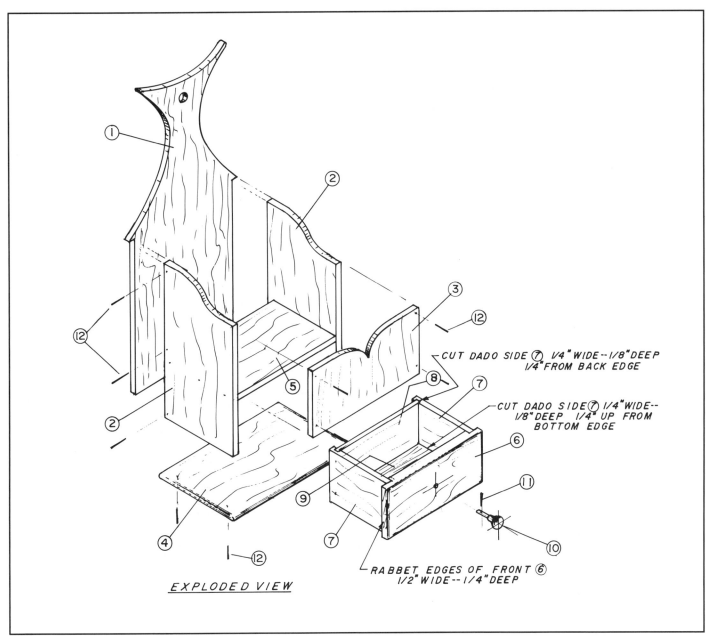

CUT DADO SIDE ⑦ 1/4" WIDE -- 1/8" DEEP
1/4" FROM BACK EDGE

CUT DADO SIDE ⑦ 1/4" WIDE --
1/8" DEEP 1/4" UP FROM
BOTTOM EDGE

RABBET EDGES OF FRONT ⑥
1/2" WIDE -- 1/4" DEEP

EXPLODED VIEW

PART	INCHES	NEEDED
1 BACK	$1/4 \times 5^{1}/_2 \times 13^{1}/_4$	1
2 SIDE	$1/4 \times 3^{1}/_4 \times 7$	2
3 FRONT	$1/4 \times 5^{1}/_2 \times 3^{1}/_2$	1
4 BOTTOM	$1/4 \times 3^{3}/_4 \times 6$	1
5 DIVIDER	$1/4 \times 3 \times 5$	1
6 DRAWER FRONT	$1/2 \times 2^{1}/_2 \times 5^{1}/_2$	1
7 DRAWER SIDE	$1/4 \times 2^{1}/_2 \times 3$	2
8 DRAWER BACK	$1/4 \times 2^{1}/_8 \times 4^{3}/_4$	1
9 DRAWER BOTTOM	$1/4 \times 3 \times 4^{3}/_4$	1
10 KNOB	$5/8$ DIA. $\times 1^{3}/_8$	1
11 PIN (FINISH NAIL)	$1/2$	1
12 SQUARE-CUT FINISH NAIL	$3/4$	AS REQ'D

Spoon Rack

In early American homes, there were few storage places for utensils, so necessity dictated the popularity of the spoon rack. This copy of an original spoon rack holds twelve spoons and makes a wonderful display for antiques. The original was painted, but it would also look great as stained, finished hardwood. Another option is to use a worn crinkle-painted finish.

Step 1. Study the plans carefully, checking the shape of each part. Visualize how you will make the spoon rack and what tools you will need.

Step 2. As you study the plans, note the order in which the project is to be assembled.

Step 3. Parts with irregular shapes or cutouts should be laid out to make a full-size pattern on a piece of heavy paper or on the wood. The drawing does not use a grid; rather, it notes the location and size of the required radius.

Step 4. Carefully cut all parts according to the materials list. Cut all parts to exact size and cut the edges exactly square (90°). Recheck all dimensions.

Step 5. Lightly sand all surfaces and edges with medium sandpaper to remove any burrs or tool marks. Keep all edges square and sharp.

Step 6. Follow the detailed illustrations and dimensions for making the parts. If you have a drill press and a ¼-inch mortise chisel (square-cut bit), use it to drill the four ¼-inch-by-½-inch slots in the three supports. If you don't have this tool, lay out the ¼-inch-by-½-inch holes and drill a series of ¼-inch-diameter holes inside the required slot. Chisel out the excess left between holes for a smooth, straight slot. Check all dimensions for accuracy. Resand with fine-grit paper, keeping all edges sharp.

Step 7. After all the pieces have been made, dry-fit them; that is, assemble the complete project without glue or nails to check for accuracy and joint fit. If any parts fit poorly, now is the time to make corrections.

Step 8. Assemble the spoon rack, keeping everything square. Check that the supports are square and nailed parallel to the backboard.

Step 9. Finish to suit, using the general finishing instructions.

Pattern begins on next page.

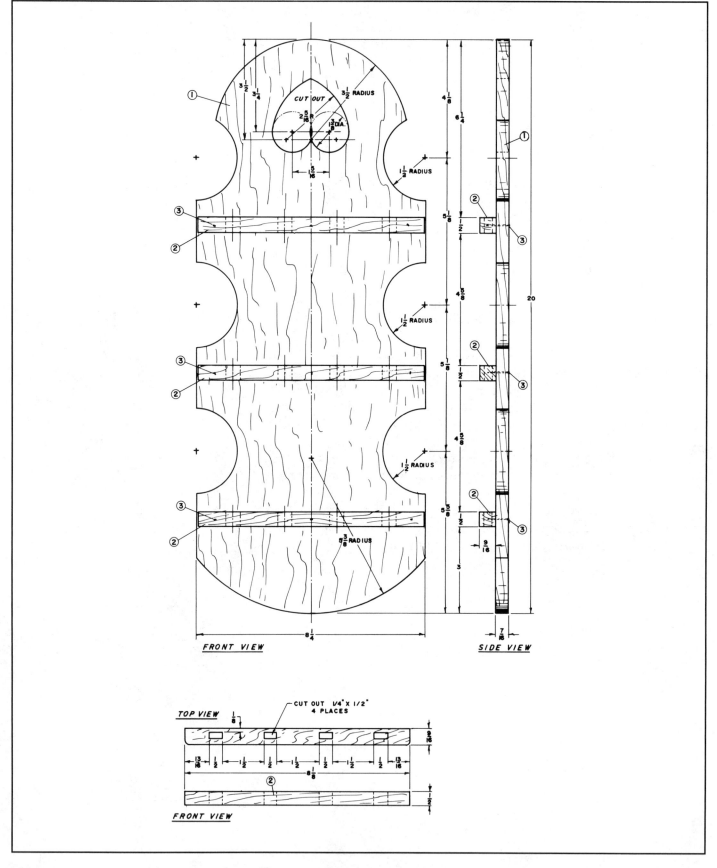

CUT OUT

3½ RADIUS

2 5/16

1⅜ DIA.

5/16

1½ RADIUS

③
②

5⅛

③
②

1½ RADIUS

4⅝

③
②

5⅛

1½ RADIUS

4⅝

③
②

5 15/16

5⅜ RADIUS

3½

3¼

3½

8¼

FRONT VIEW

4⅛

6¼

20

3

①

②

③

②

③

②

③

9/16

7/16

SIDE VIEW

CUT OUT ¼" X ½"
4 PLACES

⅛

TOP VIEW

13/16   ½   ½   ½   ½   ½   ½   13/16

8⅛

②

FRONT VIEW

½

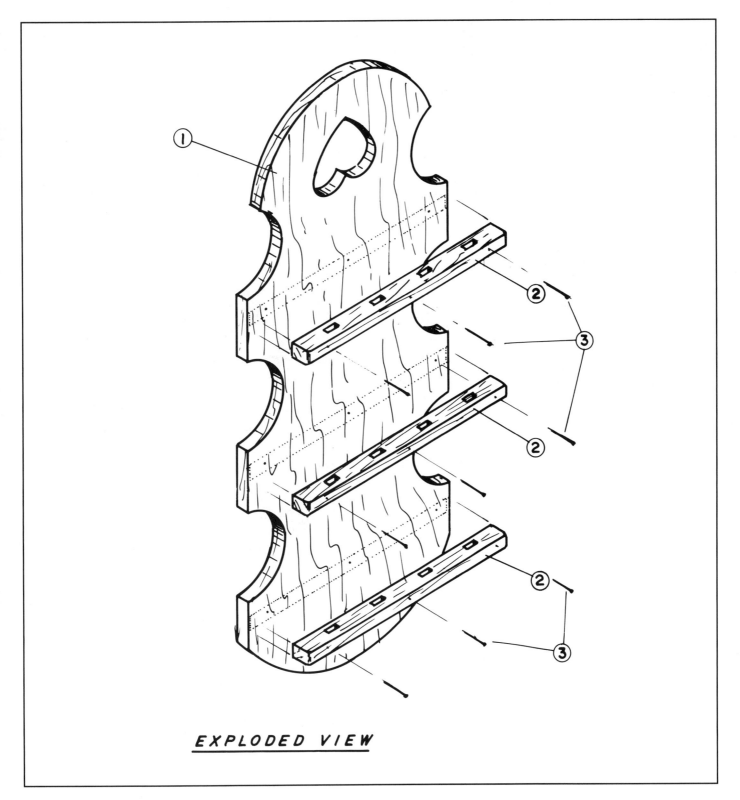

EXPLODED VIEW

PART	INCHES	NEEDED
1 BACKBOARD	$7/16 \times 8^{1}/4 \times 20$	1
2 SUPPORT	$1/2 \times 9/16 \times 8^{1}/8$	3
3 SQUARE-CUT FINISH NAIL	$7/8$	9

Candle Sconce

This candle sconce, dating to 1790, was found in Maine. The antique was made from cherry and had a pine shelf. Because it has only four pieces, it is a simple project. Use this sconce to display your candles in classic American style in any room.

Step 1. Study the plans carefully, checking the shape of each part. Visualize how you will make the candle sconce and what tools you will need.

Step 2. As you study the plans, note the order in which the project is to be assembled.

Step 3. The two parts that have irregular shapes should be laid out on a ½-inch grid to make a full-size pattern. Transfer the shape of the piece to the grid.

Step 4. Carefully cut all parts according to the materials list. Cut all parts to exact size and cut the edges exactly square (90°). Recheck all dimensions.

Step 5. Lightly sand all surfaces and edges with medium sandpaper to remove any burrs or tool marks. Keep all edges square and sharp.

Step 6. Follow the detailed illustrations and dimensions for making the parts. Set your saw at exactly 22½° when cutting the backboard (part 1) and the sides (part 2). Check all dimensions for accuracy. Resand with fine-grit paper, keeping all edges sharp.

Step 7. After all the pieces have been made, dry-fit them; that is, assemble the complete project without glue or nails to check for accuracy and joint fit. Check that the assembled parts make a perfect 90° angle. If any parts fit poorly, now is the time to make corrections.

Step 8. Assemble the candle sconce, keeping everything square. Do not let glue show on exposed surfaces.

Step 9. Finish to suit, using the general finishing instructions. I recommend a stained finish.

Pattern begins on next page.

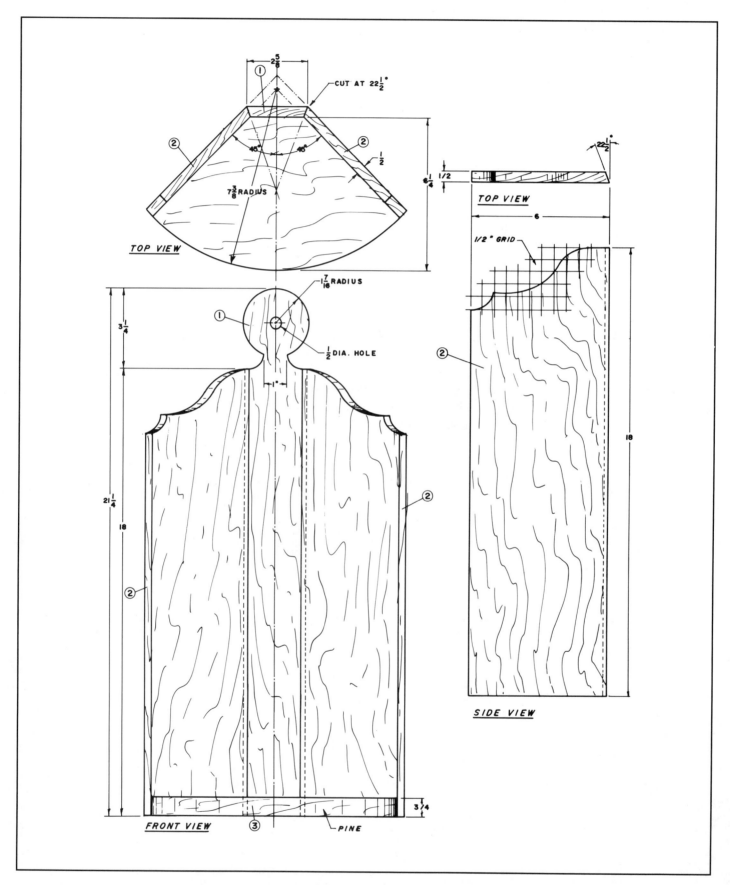

TOP VIEW

CUT AT 22½°

2⅝

①

45° 45°

7⅜ RADIUS

②   ②

½

6¼

TOP VIEW

22½°

1/2

6

1/2" GRID

②

1⁷⁄₁₆ RADIUS

①

½ DIA. HOLE

3¼

1"

②

②

21¼

18

②

18

SIDE VIEW

3/4

FRONT VIEW   ③   PINE

46

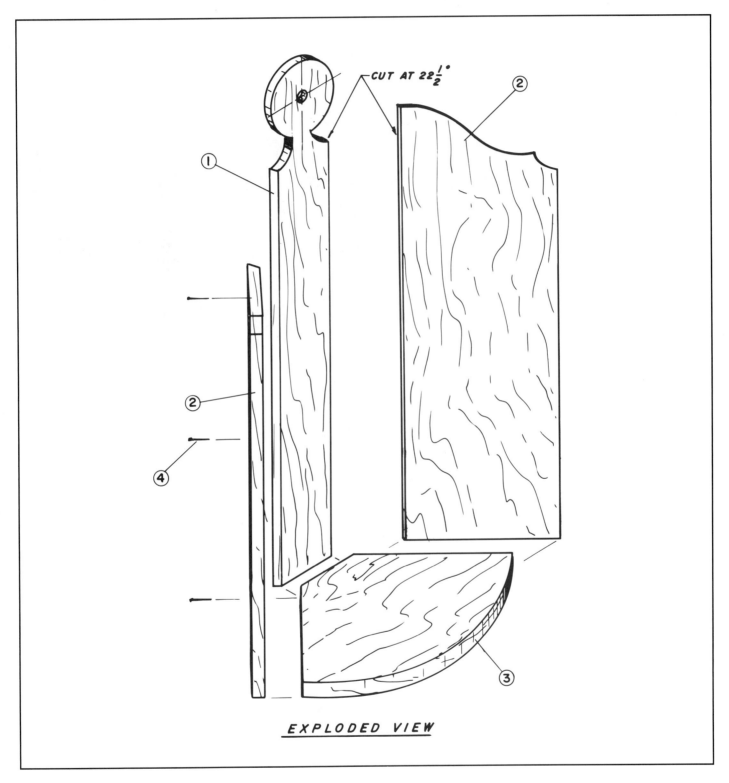

CUT AT 22$\frac{1}{2}$°

EXPLODED VIEW

PART	INCHES	NEEDED
1 BACKBOARD	$\frac{1}{8} \times 2\frac{7}{8} \times 21\frac{1}{4}$	1
2 SIDE	$\frac{1}{2} \times 6 \times 18$	2
3 BOTTOM (PINE)	$\frac{3}{4} \times 6\frac{1}{4} \times 10\frac{5}{8}$	1
4 SQUARE-CUT FINISH NAIL	$\frac{7}{8}$	10

Painted Queen Anne Planter

This planter was found in New Hampshire, painted forest green, and assembled with square-cut nails. It can be used as a wall box or to display house plants.

Step 1. Study the plans carefully, checking the shape of each part. Visualize how you will make the planter and what tools you will need.

Step 2. As you study the plans, note the order in which the project is to be assembled.

Step 3. The back (part 1) is irregular in shape, so it should be laid out to make a full-size pattern on a piece of heavy paper; then transfer the shape to the wood.

Step 4. Carefully cut all parts according to the materials list. Cut all parts to exact size and cut the edges exactly square (90°). Recheck all dimensions.

Step 5. Lightly sand all surfaces and edges with medium sandpaper to remove any burrs or tool marks. Keep all edges square and sharp.

Step 6. Follow the detailed illustrations and dimensions for making the parts. If you have a drill press, use a 3-inch-diameter sanding wheel to sand the edges of the back and sides. Check all dimensions for accuracy. Resand with fine-grit paper, keeping all edges sharp.

Step 7. After all the pieces have been made, dry-fit them; that is, assemble the complete project without glue or nails to check for accuracy and joint fit. If any parts fit poorly, now is the time to make corrections.

Step 8. Assemble the Queen Anne planter, keeping everything square. Use large square-cut nails if you have them.

Step 9. Finish to suit, using the general finishing instructions. I suggest that you paint your wall planter and give it a worn look, as pictured.

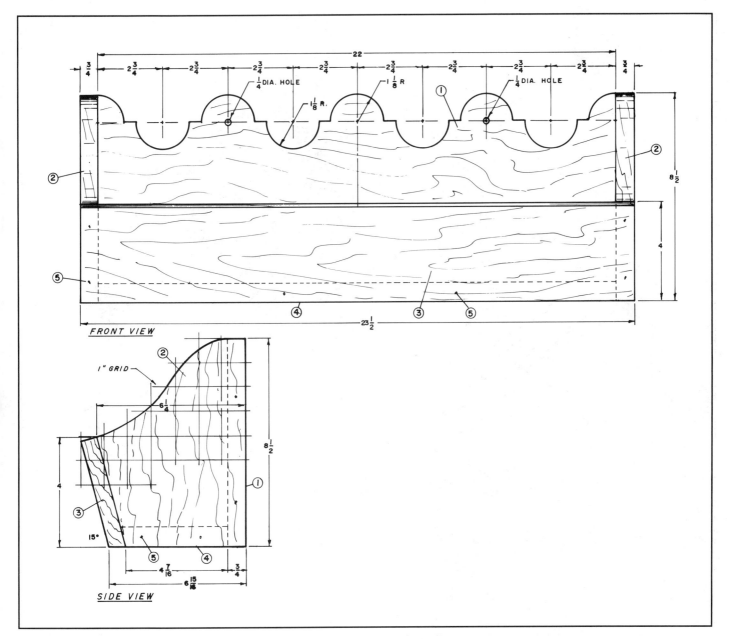

FRONT VIEW

SIDE VIEW

1" GRID

PART	INCHES	NEEDED
1 BACK	$3/4 \times 8^{1}/_2 \times 22$	1
2 SIDE	$3/4 \times 6^{1}/_4 \times 8^{1}/_2$	2
3 FRONT	$3/4 \times 4^{5}/_{16} \times 23^{1}/_2$	1
4 BOTTOM	$3/4 \times 4^{5}/_8 \times 22$	1
5 SQUARE-CUT FINISH NAIL	$1^{3}/_4$	16

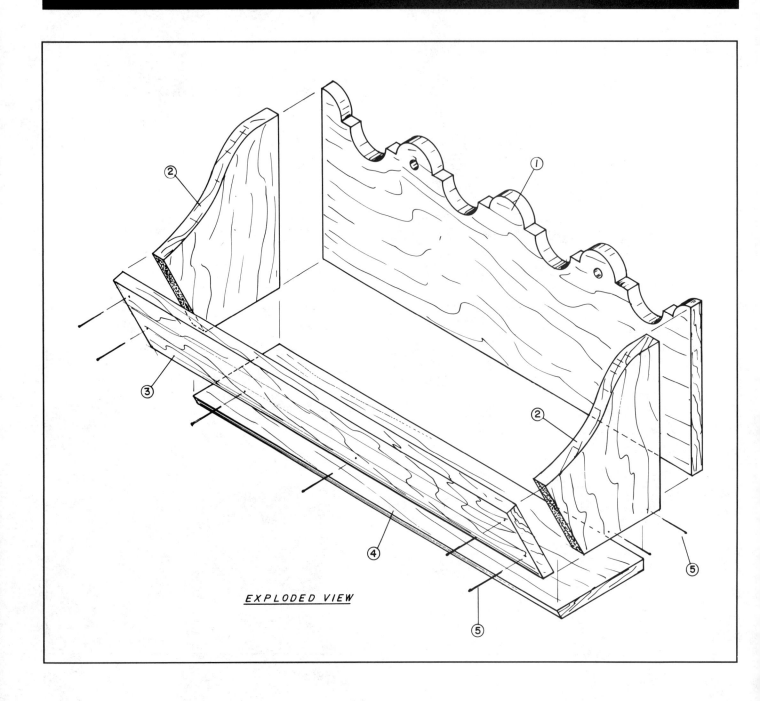

EXPLODED VIEW

50

Scroll-Top Wall Candle Box with Lid

This rare candle box, made between 1780 and 1800, was found in a southern Maine antiques shop. The original was solid mahogany with brass hinges, and its top scroll design is similar to that of the Chippendale mirrors. Use any hardwood, planed and cut to overall size. Wood can be purchased from Croffwood Mills (see the list of suppliers). Order the brass hinges (part 7) as soon as possible so they will not delay the project.

Step 1. Study the plans carefully, checking the shape of each part. Visualize how you will make the candle box and what tools you will need.

Step 2. As you study the plans, note the order in which the project is to be assembled.

Step 3. The backboard (part 1) is irregular and should be laid out on a ½-inch grid to make a full-size pattern. Transfer the shape of the piece to the grid on a heavy piece of paper or cardboard.

Step 4. Carefully cut all parts according to the materials list. Cut all parts to exact size and cut the edges exactly square (90°). Recheck all dimensions.

Step 5. Lightly sand all surfaces and edges with medium sandpaper to remove any burrs or tool marks. Keep all edges square and sharp.

Step 6. Follow the detailed illustrations and dimensions for making the parts. Check all dimensions for accuracy. Resand with fine-grit paper, keeping all edges sharp. If you have a parallel arm scroll saw, the backboard will be easy to cut. A band saw with a thin blade or saber saw will also work well. If you don't have any power tools, use a jigsaw, as the original craftsmen did.

Step 7. After all the pieces have been made, dry-fit them; that is, assemble the complete project without glue or nails to check for accuracy and joint fit. If any parts fit poorly, now is the time to make corrections.

Step 8. Assemble the candle box, keeping everything square. Temporarily attach the hinges; remove them before adding the stain or finish coats.

Step 10. Finish to suit, using the general finishing instructions. I recommend a stained and satin finish.

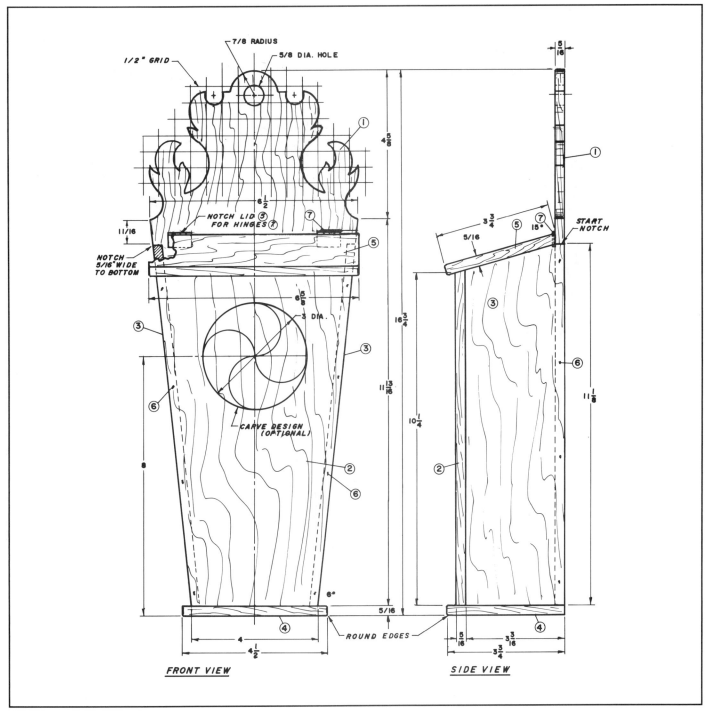

PART	INCHES	NEEDED
1 BACKBOARD	$5/16 \times 6^5/8 \times 16^7/16$	1
2 FRONT	$5/16 \times 6^5/16 \times 10^5/16$	1
3 SIDE	$5/16 \times 3^3/16 \times 11^1/8$	2
4 BOTTOM	$5/16 \times 3^3/4 \times 4^1/2$	1
5 LID	$5/16 \times 3^3/4 \times 6^5/8$	1
6 SQUARE-CUT FINISH NAIL	$3/4$	20
7 HINGE (BRASS)	$3/4 \times 3/4$	2

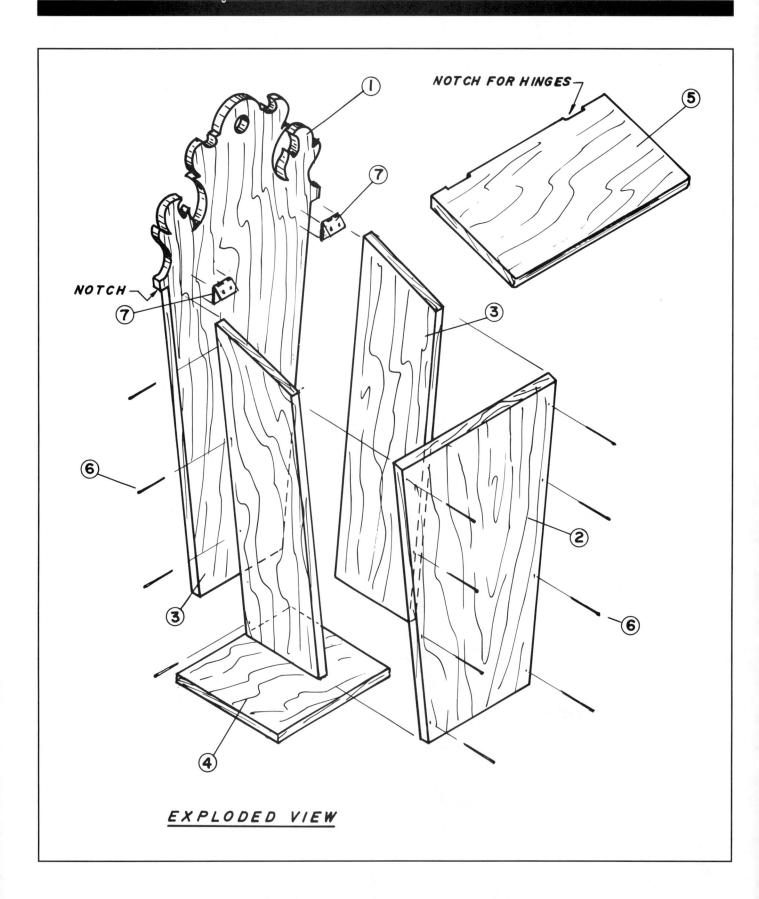

NOTCH FOR HINGES

NOTCH

EXPLODED VIEW

Small Queen Anne Mirror

Many small mirrors were made in Colonial America, but this example has exceptionally beautiful, graceful lines. To obtain the exact profile, order a special router cutter bit from Cascade Tools, Inc. (see the list of suppliers). You can approximate the illustrated shape, however, by using a combination of standard router bits. Anything close will work—only you will know it is not exact. If you have a parallel-arm scroll saw, this project will be very simple to complete. It can also be cut using a hand jigsaw or saber saw. Purchase the glass after you make the mirror frame so that your measurements will be exact.

Step 1. Study the plans carefully, checking the shape of each part. Visualize how you will make the Queen Anne mirror and what tools you will need.

Step 2. As you study the plans, note the order in which the project is to be assembled.

Step 3. Because the mirror has an irregular shape, it should be laid out on a ½-inch grid to make a full-size pattern on heavy paper or cardboard. Transfer the shape of the mirror to the grid.

Step 4. Carefully cut all parts according to the materials list. Cut all parts to exact size and cut the edges exactly square (90°). Recheck all dimensions.

Step 5. Lightly sand all surfaces and edges with medium sandpaper to remove any burrs or tool marks. Keep all edges square and sharp.

Step 6. Follow the detailed illustrations and dimensions for making the parts. A router table simplifies cutting the molding. Check all dimensions for accuracy. Resand with fine-grit paper, keeping all edges sharp.

Step 7. After all the pieces have been made, dry-fit them; that is, assemble the complete project without glue or nails to check for accuracy and joint fit. If any parts fit poorly, now is the time to make corrections.

Step 8. Glue the top and bottom to the sides, keeping the angle exactly 90°. After the frame is glued, cut a notch ³/₁₆-inch wide by ¼-inch deep across the top edge for the scroll.

Step 9. Cut the backboard (part 7) slightly smaller than the opening. Cut the backboard's four edges at 15° as shown. Note that the size of the mirror should be the same as that of the backboard.

Step 10. Finish to suit, using the general finishing instructions.

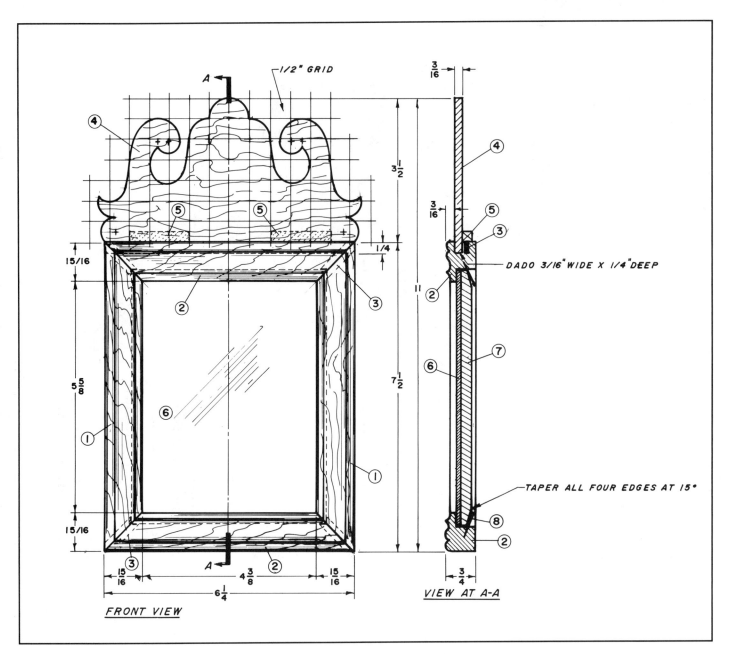

FRONT VIEW

VIEW AT A-A

1/2" GRID

DADO 3/16" WIDE X 1/4" DEEP

TAPER ALL FOUR EDGES AT 15°

PART	INCHES	NEEDED
1 SIDE	$3/4 \times 15/16 \times 7 1/2$	2
2 TOP, BOTTOM	$3/4 \times 15/16 \times 6 1/4$	2
3 SPLINE	$1/8 \times 1/4 \times 15/16$	4
4 TOP SCROLL	$3/16 \times 3 3/4 \times 6 1/2$	1
5 BLOCK	$1/4 \times 1/4 \times 1 1/2$	2
6 MIRROR	$3/32 \times 4 7/8 \times 6 1/8$	1
7 BACKBOARD	$1/4 \times 4 7/8 \times 6 1/8$	1
8 SQUARE-CUT FINISH NAIL	$3/4$	4

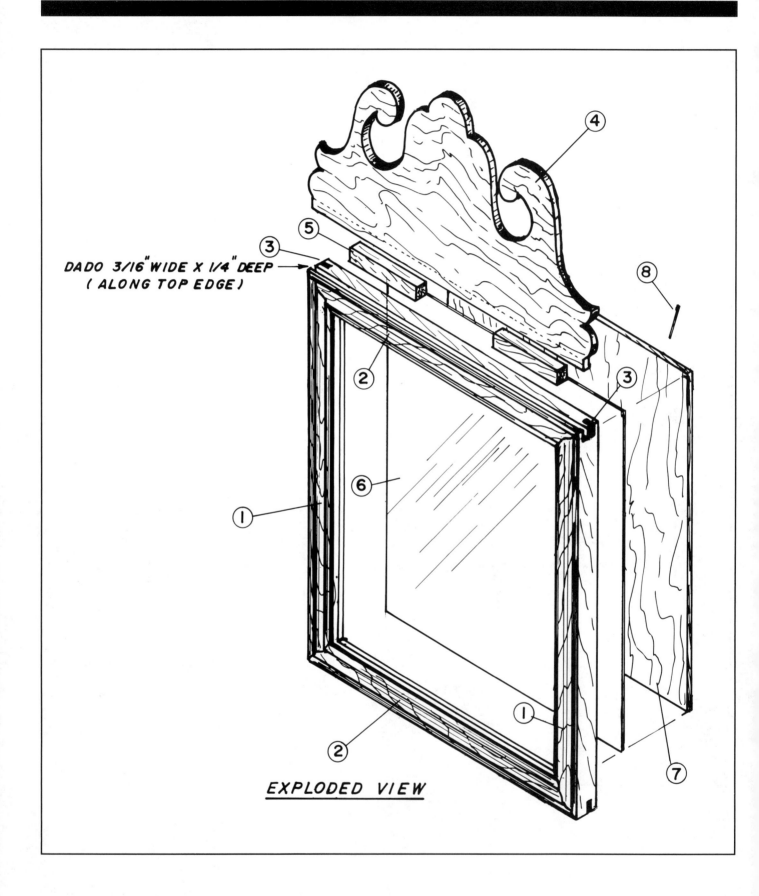

DADO 3/16" WIDE X 1/4" DEEP
(ALONG TOP EDGE)

EXPLODED VIEW

58

Pennsylvania Salt Crystal Wall Box with Lid

Housed in the Metropolitan Museum of Art, this popular 1750 salt crystal wall box was made of pine and painted red. The copy pictured was made of cherry and left unpainted. The side of this wall box has unusual lines, perhaps adding to its attraction. Although the original box is very large, you might want scale it down; for a box 15 inches high, use a grid with ¾-inch squares.

Step 1. Study the plans carefully, checking the shape of each part. Visualize how you will make the wall box and what tools you will need.

Step 2. As you study the plans, note the order in which the project is to be assembled.

Step 3. The sides (part 2) are irregular and should be laid out on a 1-inch grid to make a full-size pattern. Transfer the shape of the piece to the grid, and then trace it on the wood.

Step 4. Carefully cut all parts according to the materials list. Cut all parts to exact size and cut the edges exactly square (90°). Recheck all dimensions.

Step 5. Lightly sand all surfaces and edges with medium sandpaper to remove any burrs or tool marks. Keep all edges square and sharp.

Step 6. Follow the detailed illustrations and dimensions for making the parts. Tape the sides together before cutting them out so that you will have a perfect match. Check all dimensions for accuracy. Resand with fine-grit paper, keeping all edges sharp.

Step 7. After all the pieces have been made, dry-fit them; that is, assemble the complete project without glue or nails to check for accuracy and joint fit. If any parts fit poorly, now is the time to make corrections.

Step 8. Assemble the salt crystal wall box, keeping everything square. Temporarily attach the hinges; remove them before adding the stain or finish coats.

Step 10. Finish to suit, using the general finishing instructions.

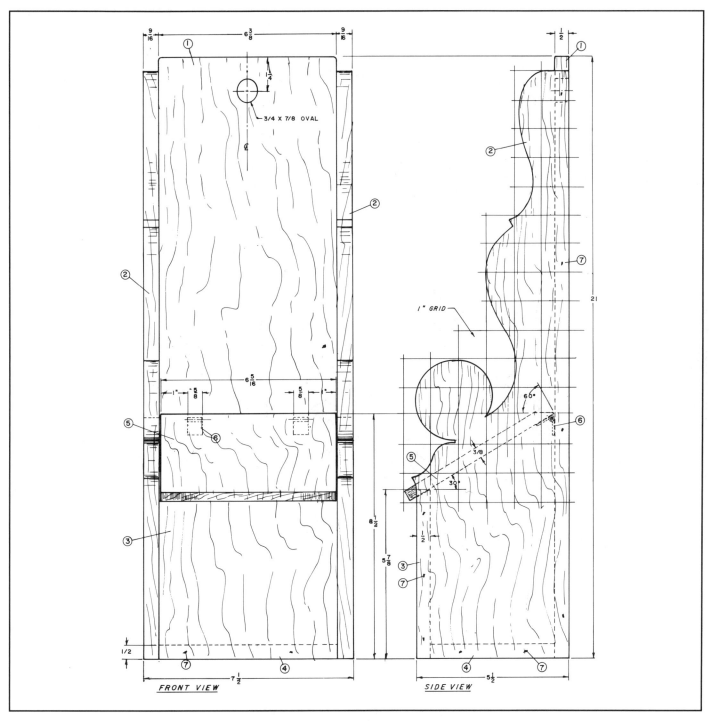

PART	INCHES	NEEDED
1 BACK	$1/2 \times 6^3/8 \times 21$	1
2 SIDE	$9/16 \times 5^3/4 \times 20^1/2$	2
3 FRONT	$1/2 \times 6^3/8 \times 5^7/8$	3
4 BOTTOM	$1/2 \times 4^1/2 \times 6^1/2$	1
5 LID	$3/8 \times 6^7/16 \times 6$	1
6 HINGE	$5/8$ WIDE	2
7 SQUARE-CUT FINISH NAIL	1	16

61

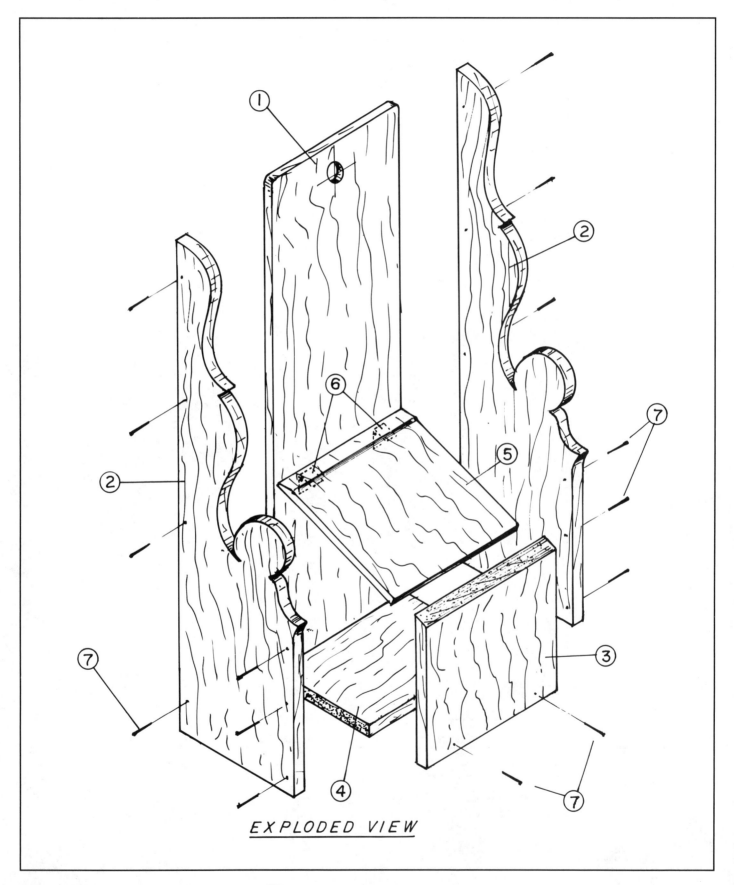

EXPLODED VIEW

Formal Wall Box with Drawer

This box, made of solid walnut, was found in a northern Massachusetts antiques shop, selling for $575. The price indicates that it is unusual; however, I don't know what it was used for. It is shaped like a pipe box with Queen Anne lines, and the drawer pull was hand carved. You may want to purchase a pull rather than carve one.

Step 1. Study the plans carefully, checking the shape of each part. Visualize how you will make the formal wall box and its drawer, and what tools you will need.

Step 2. As you study the plans, note the order in which the project is to be assembled.

Step 3. Because the back, front, and sides have irregular shapes, they should be laid out on a ½-inch grid to make a full-size pattern on heavy paper or cardboard. Transfer the shape of each piece to the grid, then trace it on the wood.

Step 4. Carefully cut all parts according to the materials list. Cut all parts to exact size and cut the edges exactly square (90°). Recheck all dimensions.

Step 5. Lightly sand all surfaces and edges with medium sandpaper to remove any burrs or tool marks. Keep all edges square and sharp.

Step 6. Follow the detailed illustrations and dimensions for making the parts. Check all dimensions for accuracy. Tape the sides together before cutting them out so you will have a perfect match. Cut out the opening for the drawer, remembering to account for the drawer's lip on the side and top edges. Resand with fine-grit paper, keeping all edges sharp.

Step 7. After all the pieces have been made, dry-fit them; that is, assemble the complete project without glue or nails to check for accuracy and joint fit. Check that the drawer fits correctly. If any parts fit poorly, now is the time to make corrections.

Step 8. Assemble the formal wall box, keeping everything square.

Step 9. Finish to suit, using the general finishing instructions.

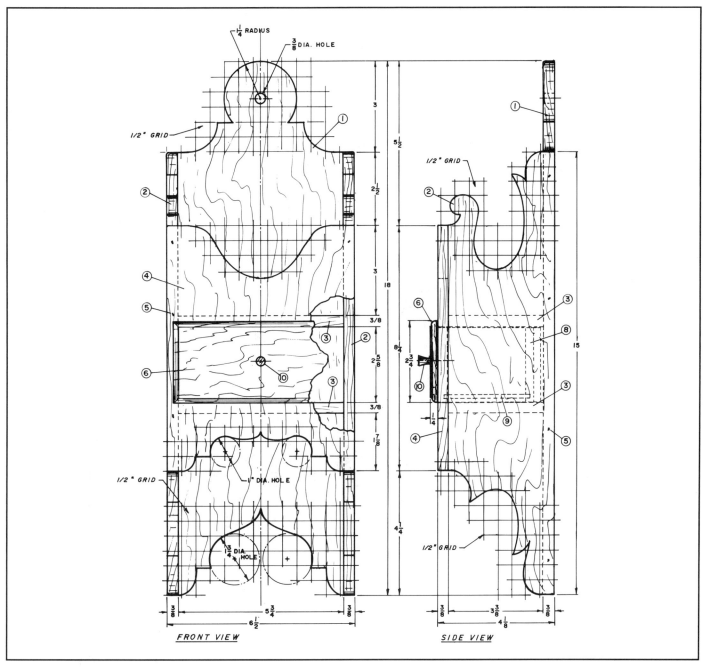

FRONT VIEW   SIDE VIEW

	PART	INCHES	NEEDED
1	BACK	$3/8 \times 5^3/4 \times 18$	1
2	SIDE	$3/8 \times 3^3/4 \times 15$	2
3	SHELF	$3/8 \times 3^3/8 \times 5^3/4$	2
4	FRONT	$3/8 \times 6^1/2 \times 8^1/4$	1
5	SQUARE-CUT FINISH NAIL	$3/4$	AS REQ'D
6	DRAWER FRONT	$5/8 \times 2^3/4 \times 6$	1
7	DRAWER SIDE	$1/4 \times 2^1/2 \times 3^5/8$	2
8	DRAWER BACK	$1/4 \times 2^1/2 \times 5^1/2$	1
9	DRAWER BOTTOM	$1/8 \times 3^1/4 \times 5^1/2$	1
10	PULL	$3/8$ DIA. $\times 1$	1

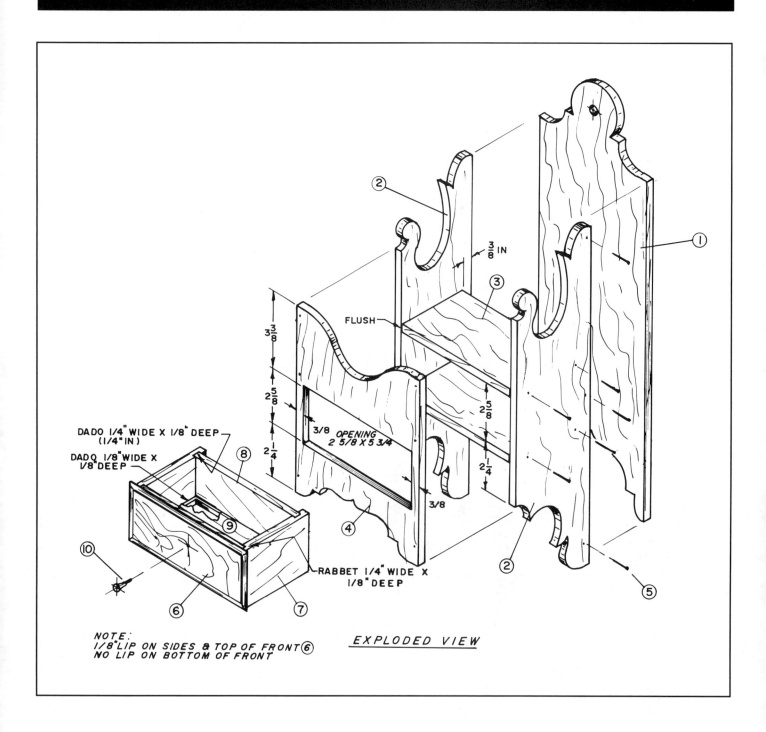

DADO 1/4" WIDE X 1/8" DEEP
(1/4" IN)

DADO 1/8" WIDE X
1/8" DEEP

⑧

⑨

⑩

⑥

⑦

RABBET 1/4" WIDE X
1/8" DEEP

NOTE:
1/8" LIP ON SIDES & TOP OF FRONT ⑥
NO LIP ON BOTTOM OF FRONT

②

$\frac{3}{8}$ IN

③

FLUSH

$3\frac{3}{8}$

$2\frac{5}{8}$

$2\frac{1}{4}$

3/8 OPENING
2 5/8 X 5 3/4

④

$2\frac{5}{8}$

$2\frac{1}{4}$

3/8

②

①

⑤

EXPLODED VIEW

Large New England Wall Box

This version of a wall box is much larger than most, so you may want to scale it down. It has the unique feature of a 1-inch ogee trim cut on two sides. The original was painted, but you may decide to use a crinkle finish instead.

Step 1. Study the plans carefully, checking the shape of each part. Visualize how you will make the large wall box and what tools you will need.

Step 2. As you study the plans, note the order in which the project is to be assembled.

Step 3. Because the back and sides have irregular shapes, they should be laid out on a 1-inch grid to make a full-size pattern on heavy paper or cardboard. Transfer the shape of each piece to the grid, then trace it on the wood.

Step 4. Carefully cut all parts according to the materials list. Cut all parts to exact size and cut the edges exactly square (90°). Recheck all dimensions.

Step 5. Lightly sand all surfaces and edges with medium sandpaper to remove any burrs or tool marks. Keep all edges square and sharp.

Step 6. Follow the detailed illustrations and dimensions for making the parts. Check all dimensions for accuracy. When you cut the 1-inch ogee trim on the tip of the sides, be sure to cut matching sides (not two right sides). Resand with fine-grit paper, keeping all edges sharp.

Step 7. After all the pieces have been made, dry-fit them; that is, assemble the complete project without glue or nails to check for accuracy and joint fit. If any parts fit poorly, now is the time to make corrections.

Step 8. Assemble the New England wall box, keeping everything square. Leave the large square-cut nails showing.

Step 9. Finish to suit, using the general finishing instructions.

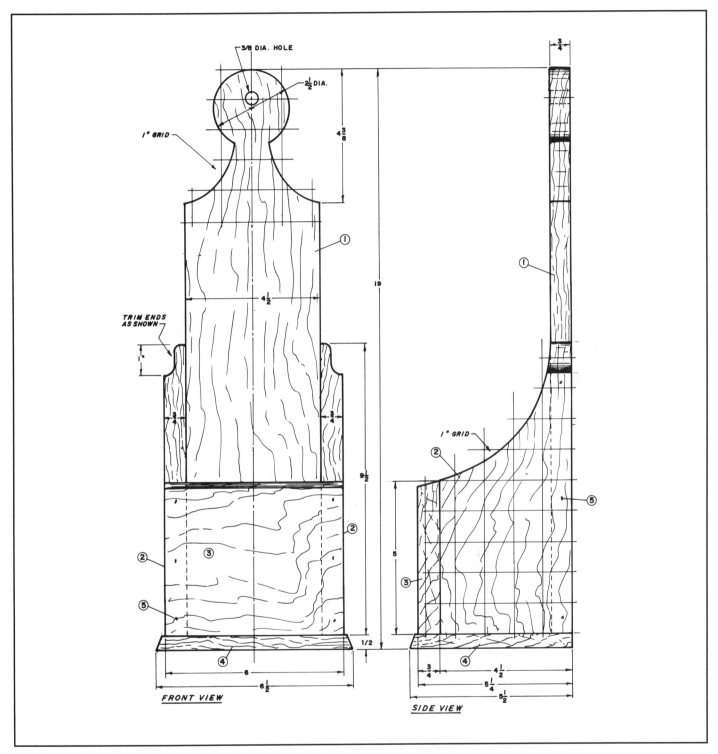

3/8 DIA. HOLE

2 1/2 DIA.

1" GRID

3/4

4 3/8

19

1

4 1/2

TRIM ENDS AS SHOWN

3/4

3/4

9 1/2

2

2

3

1" GRID

2

1

5

5

3

3

5

1/2

4

4

6

3/4

4 1/2

6 1/2

5 1/4

5 1/2

FRONT VIEW

SIDE VIEW

PART	INCHES	NEEDED
1 BACK	$3/4 \times 4 1/2 \times 18 1/2$	1
2 SIDE	$3/4 \times 4 1/2 \times 9 1/2$	2
3 FRONT	$3/4 \times 5 \times 6$	1
4 BOTTOM	$1/2 \times 5 1/2 \times 6 1/2$	1
5 SQUARE-CUT FINISH NAIL	$1 1/2$	16

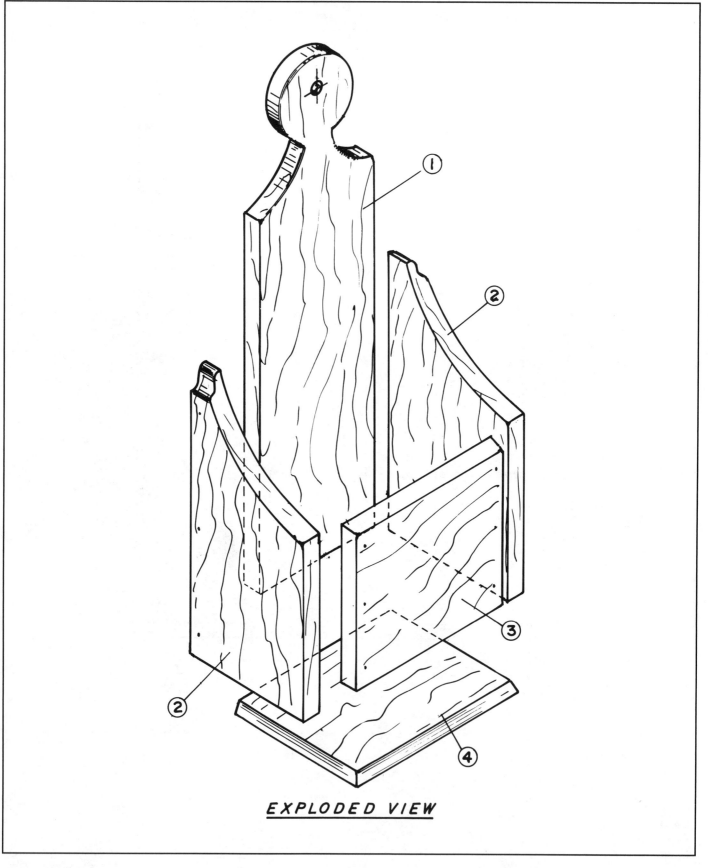

EXPLODED VIEW

Shelf Watch Hutch

The original of this unusual hutch, made of mahogany, was designed to look like a formal federal shelf clock. It is the perfect place to display your family heirloom watch. The copy pictured was distressed and aged.

Step 1. Study the plans carefully, checking the shape of each part. Visualize how you will make the shelf watch hutch and what tools you will need.

Step 2. As you study the plans, note the order in which the project is to be assembled.

Step 3. Turn the columns first and build the hutch around them. If you do not have a lathe, contact Riverbend Turnings (see the list of suppliers) for custom-turned columns.

Step 4. Carefully cut all parts according to the materials list. Cut all parts to exact size and cut the edges exactly square (90°). Recheck all dimensions.

Step 5. Lightly sand all surfaces and edges with medium sandpaper to remove any burrs or tool marks. Keep all edges square and sharp.

Step 6. Follow the detailed illustrations and dimensions for making the parts. Check all dimensions for accuracy. Resand with fine-grit paper, keeping all edges sharp.

Step 7. After all the pieces have been made, dry-fit them; that is, assemble the complete project without glue or nails to check for accuracy and joint fit. If any parts fit poorly, now is the time to make corrections.

Step 8. Glue together the top and bottom moldings first and then add the box body and the two columns. Stick to the given dimensions so that the pieces will fit together the first time.

Step 9. Finish to suit, using the general finishing instructions.

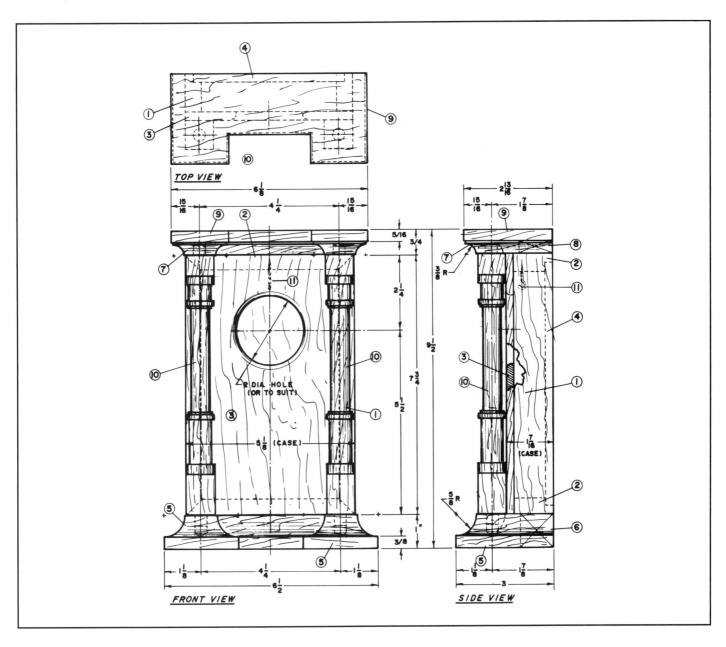

PART		INCHES	NEEDED
1	FRAME—STILE	$1/2 \times 1^{3}/_{16} \times 7^{3}/_{4}$	2
2	FRAME—RAIL	$1/2 \times 1^{3}/_{16} \times 5^{1}/_{8}$	2
3	FACE	$1/4 \times 5^{1}/_{8} \times 7^{3}/_{4}$	1
4	BACK	$1/4 \times 4^{5}/_{8} \times 7^{1}/_{2}$	1
5	BASE MOLDING	$1 \times 1^{1}/_{8} \times 24$, cut to size	1
6	FILLER BASE	$1 \times 1 \times 4^{1}/_{4}$	1
7	TOP MOLDING	$7/_{16} \times 7/_{8} \times 24$, cut to size	1
8	FILLER TOP	$7/_{16} \times 1 \times 4^{1}/_{4}$	1
9	TOP BOARD	$5/_{16} \times 2^{13}/_{16} \times 6^{1}/_{8}$	1
10	COLUMN	$7/_{8}$ SQ. $\times 8^{1}/_{2}$	2
11	HOOK (BRASS)	TO SUIT	1
12	ROUND-HEAD SCREW	NO. 6—$3/_{4}$ LONG BRASS	2

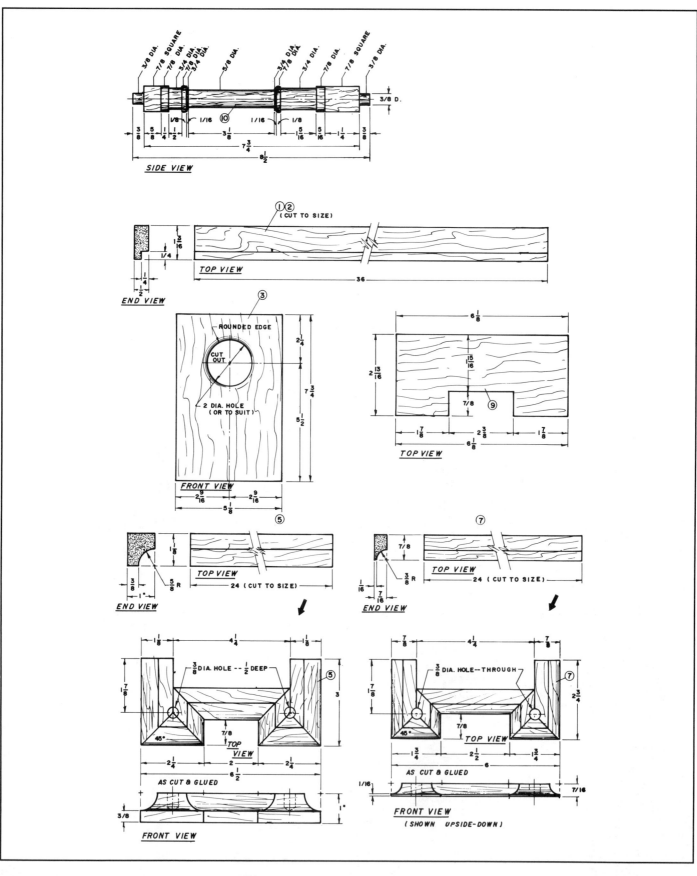

SIDE VIEW

TOP VIEW

END VIEW

FRONT VIEW

TOP VIEW

END VIEW

END VIEW

FRONT VIEW

FRONT VIEW
(SHOWN UPSIDE-DOWN)

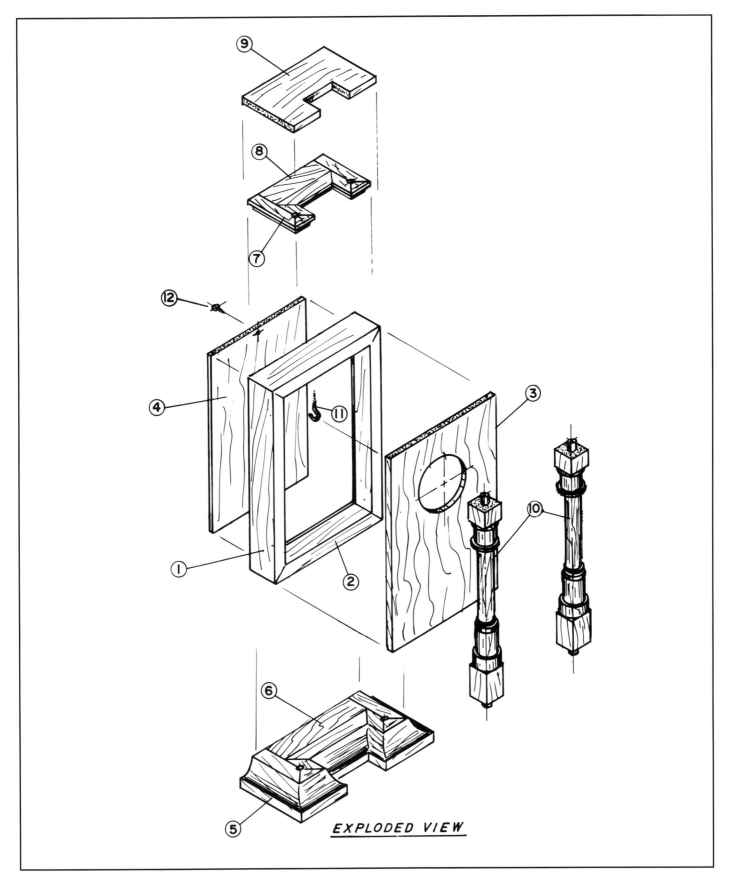

EXPLODED VIEW

Footstool

Footstools came in many shapes and sizes; I have never seen two alike. Many early settlers made their own version of a footstool, or cricket, with a hammer and saw. Most were made with a simple butt joint construction. Many Vermont footstools had painted braces and legs but stained and finished tops. Of all the footstools I've made, I think this walnut one has the best lines and proportions.

Step 1. Study the plans carefully, checking the shape of each part. Visualize how you will make the footstool and what tools you will need.

Step 2. As you study the plans, note the order in which the project is to be assembled.

Step 3. Because the brace and legs have irregular shapes, they should be laid out on a ½-inch grid to make a full-size pattern on heavy paper or cardboard. Transfer the shape of each piece to the grid.

Step 4. Carefully cut all parts according to the materials list. Cut all parts to exact size and cut the edges exactly square (90°). Recheck all dimensions.

Step 5. Lightly sand all surfaces and edges with medium sandpaper to remove any burrs or tool marks. Keep all edges square and sharp.

Step 6. Follow the detailed illustrations and dimensions for making the parts. Check all dimensions for accuracy. Tape the two legs and braces together before cutting them out, so that you have exact pairs. Resand with fine-grit paper, keeping all edges sharp.

Step 7. After all the pieces have been made, dry-fit them; that is, assemble the complete project without glue or nails to check for accuracy and joint fit. If any parts fit poorly, now is the time to make corrections.

Step 8. Assemble the footstool, keeping everything square.

Step 9. Finish to suit, using the general finishing instructions.

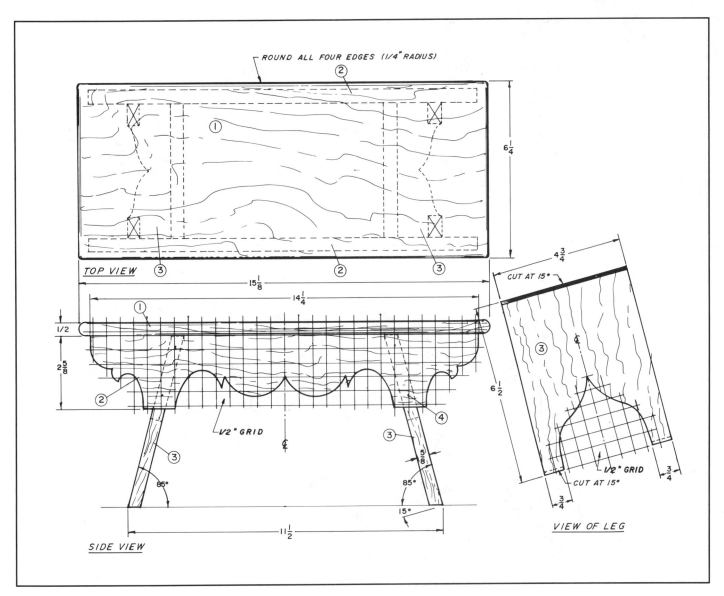

ROUND ALL FOUR EDGES (1/4" RADIUS)

TOP VIEW

SIDE VIEW

VIEW OF LEG

CUT AT 15°

1/2" GRID

PART	INCHES	NEEDED
1 TOP BOARD	$1/2 \times 6^{1}/_4 \times 15^{1}/_8$	1
2 BRACE	$1/2 \times 2^{5}/_8 \times 14^{1}/_4$	2
3 LEG	$5/8 \times 4^{3}/_4 \times 6^{1}/_2$	2
4 SQUARE-CUT FINISH NAIL	$1^{3}/_4$	8

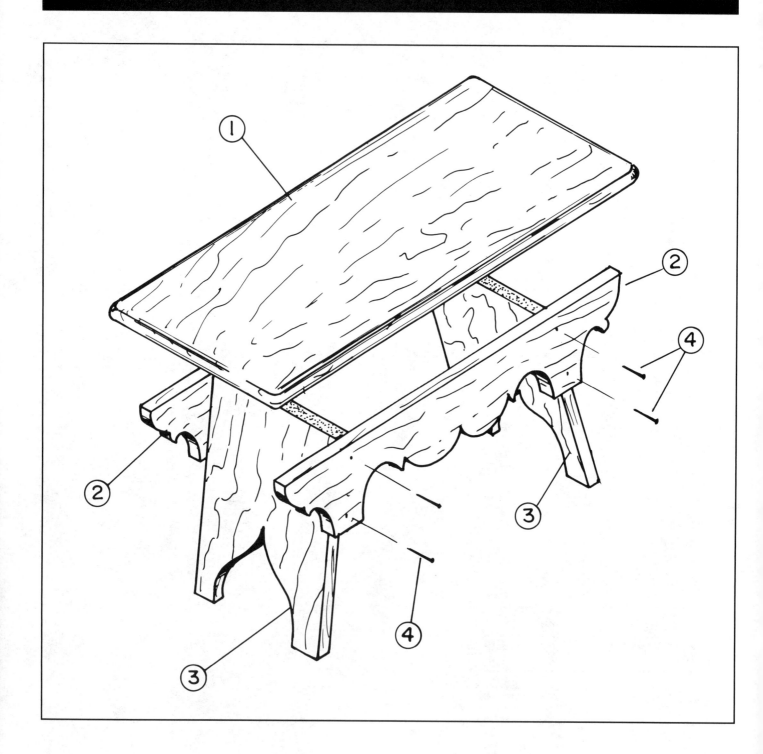

English Pipe Box

This 1750 walnut pipe box has a tray style unlike the common wall-hanging version. Its handle divides the box into two compartments for long clay pipes, and the lidded areas were used to store tobacco. Because walnut is not available at most lumberyards, you may need to obtain the wood from one of the suppliers listed.

Step 1. Study the plans carefully, checking the shape of each part. Visualize how you will make the pipe box and what tools you will need.

Step 2. As you study the plans, note the order in which the project is to be assembled.

Step 3. Because the divider has an irregular shape, it should be laid out on a 1-inch grid to make a full-size pattern on heavy paper or cardboard. Transfer the shape of each piece to the grid, then trace it on the wood.

Step 4. Carefully cut all parts according to the materials list. Cut all parts to exact size and cut the edges exactly square (90°). Recheck all dimensions.

Step 5. Lightly sand all surfaces and edges with medium sandpaper to remove any burrs or tool marks. Keep all edges square and sharp.

Step 6. Follow the detailed illustrations and dimensions for making the parts. Check all dimensions for accuracy. Resand with fine-grit paper, keeping all edges sharp.

Step 7. After all the pieces have been made, dry-fit them; that is, assemble the complete project without glue or nails to check for accuracy and joint fit. If any parts fit poorly, now is the time to make corrections.

Step 8. Assemble the English pipe box, keeping everything square.

Step 9. Finish to suit, using the general finishing instructions.

Pattern begins on next page.

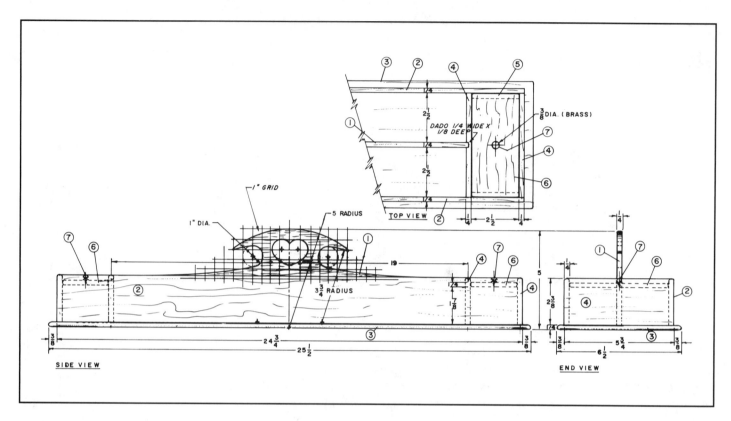

PART	INCHES	NEEDED
1 DIVIDER HANDLE	$1/4 \times 4^3/4 \times 19$	1
2 SIDE	$1/4 \times 2^3/8 \times 24^3/4$	2
3 BASE	$1/4 \times 6^1/2 \times 25^1/2$	1
4 END, DIVIDER	$1/4 \times 2^3/8 \times 5^1/4$	4
5 LID SUPPORT	$1/4 \times 1^7/8 \times 2^1/2$	4
6 LID	$1/4 \times 2^1/2 \times 5^1/4$	2
7 KNOB (BRASS)	$3/8$ DIA.	2

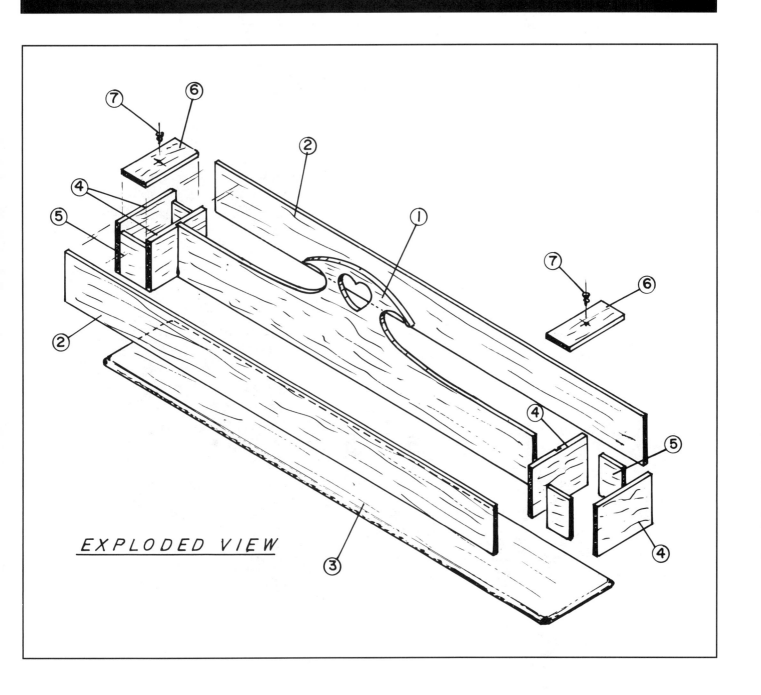

EXPLODED VIEW

Hooded Cradle

Deborah Porter

Because people in Colonial America believed the night air was unhealthy, they built cradles with solid sides, side wings, and hoods to shield their babies from drafts. On the sides of some early cradles were wooden knobs to button or tie down a coverlet; other cradles had handholds on their sides for portability. Cradles were rocked with the foot so that hands could be free for other tasks.

This model rocks from side to side, as did most. Some people, however, hoping to prevent colic, positioned the rockers so that the cradle would rock from head to foot. This pine cradle has the traditional lines of those built in the 1800s. Oddly, rockers were added to cradles circa 1400—about four hundred years before anyone thought to add rockers to chairs for adults.

Step 1. Study the plans carefully, checking the shape of each part. Visualize how you will make the hooded cradle and what tools you will need.

Step 2. As you study the plans, note the order in which the project is to be assembled.

Step 3. Because the wing and rocker have irregular shapes, they should be laid out on a ½-inch grid to make a full-size pattern on heavy paper or cardboard. Transfer the shape of each piece to the grid.

Step 4. Carefully cut all parts according to the materials list. Cut all parts to exact size and cut the edges exactly square (90°). Recheck all dimensions.

Step 5. Lightly sand all surfaces and edges with medium sandpaper to remove any burrs or tool marks. Keep all edges square and sharp.

Step 6. Follow the detailed illustrations and dimensions for making the parts. Check all dimensions for accuracy. Cut a smooth arc with no flat areas on the rocker. Make mirror-image sides for the right and left. Resand with fine-grit paper, keeping all edges sharp.

Step 7. After all the pieces have been made, dry-fit them; that is, assemble the complete project without glue or nails to check for accuracy and joint fit. If any parts fit poorly, now is the time to make corrections.

Step 8. Assemble the hooded cradle, keeping everything square.

Step 9. Finish to suit, using the general finishing instructions.

Pattern begins on next page.

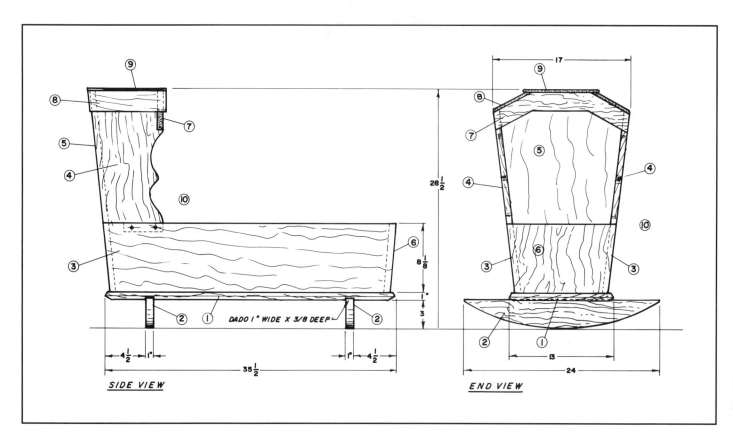

SIDE VIEW

END VIEW

	PART	INCHES	NEEDED
1	PLATFORM	$1 \times 13 \times 35^{1/2}$	1
2	ROCKER	$1 \times 3^{3/8} \times 24$	2
3	SIDE	$^{3/4} \times 8^{1/4} \times 36^{1/2}$	2
4	WING	$^{3/4} \times 9 \times 14$	2
5	BACK	$^{3/4} \times 17 \times 24$	1
6	FOOT BOARD	$^{3/4} \times 13^{3/4} \times 8^{1/4}$	1
7	ROOF SUPPORT	$^{3/4} \times 4^{1/2} \times 17$	1
8	ROOF SIDE	$^{3/8} \times 5^{3/4} \times 9^{3/4}$	2
9	ROOF TOP	$^{3/8} \times 9^{3/8} \times 9^{3/4}$	1
10	PIN	$^{1/4}$ DIA. $\times ^{3/4}$	4
11	SQUARE-CUT FINISH NAIL	$1^{1/2}$	AS REQ'D

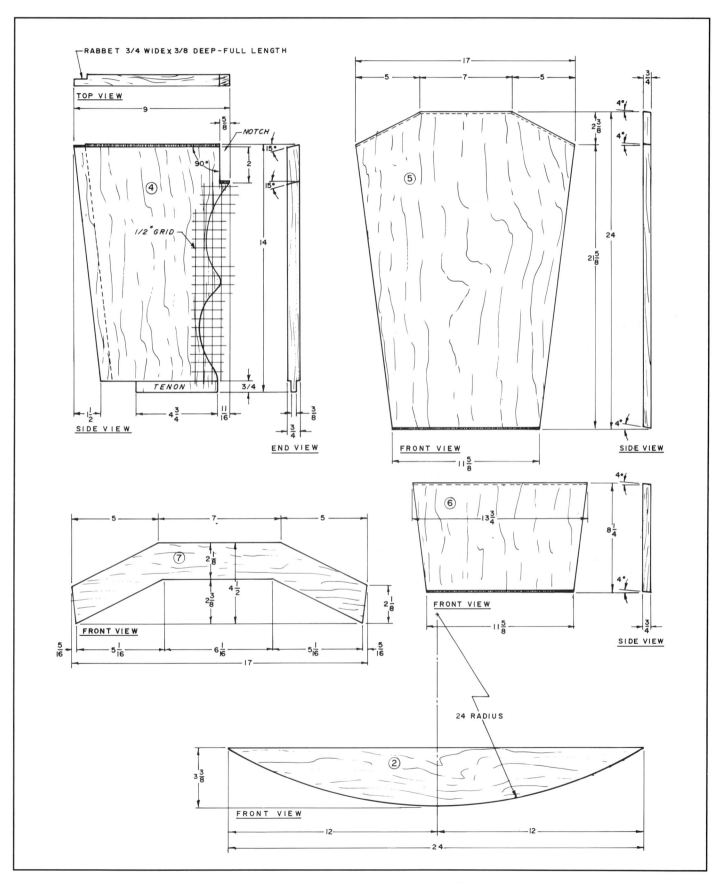

RABBET 3/4 WIDE x 3/8 DEEP - FULL LENGTH

TOP VIEW

9

⑤

⑦

⑥

② 24 RADIUS

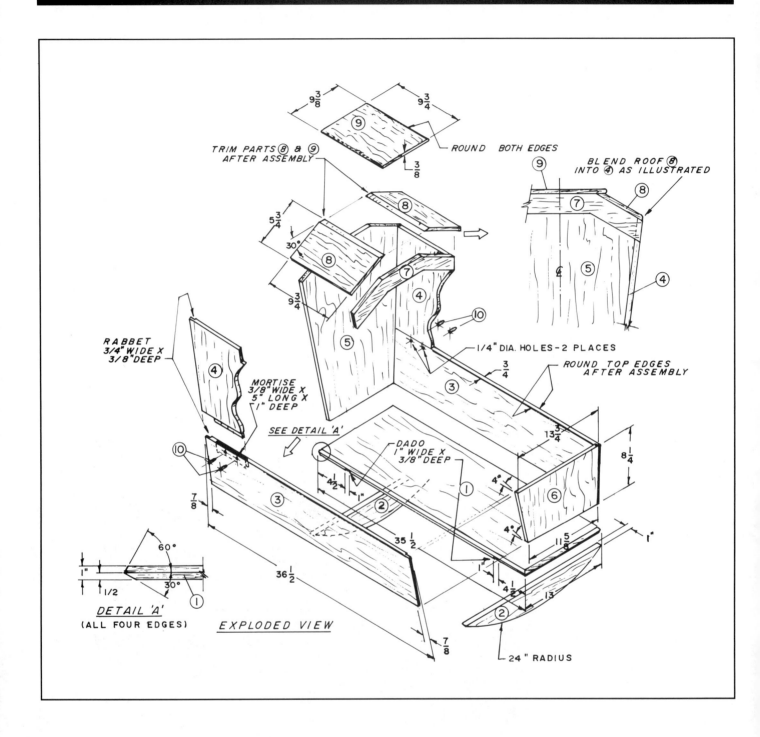

TRIM PARTS ⑧ & ⑨
AFTER ASSEMBLY

⑨ 9¾

⑨ 9¾

ROUND BOTH EDGES

3/8

BLEND ROOF ⑧
INTO ④ AS ILLUSTRATED

⑧ ⑨ ⑦ ⑧

5¾

30°

⑧ ⑦ ④

④ ⑤

3/4 9

⑤

⑩

⑤ ④

RABBET
3/4" WIDE X
3/8" DEEP

④

1/4" DIA. HOLES - 2 PLACES

3/4

③

ROUND TOP EDGES
AFTER ASSEMBLY

MORTISE
3/8" WIDE X
5" LONG X
1" DEEP

SEE DETAIL 'A'

DADO
1" WIDE X
3/8" DEEP

13¾

8¼

⑩

7/8

4½ 1"

③ ② ①

4°

⑥

4°

11⅝

35½

1"

60°

1"

1/2 30°

①

DETAIL 'A'
(ALL FOUR EDGES)

EXPLODED VIEW

36½

7/8

4½

13

②

24" RADIUS

86

Child's Rocking Chair

The rocking chair, an American invention, is often attributed to Benjamin Franklin, who began making them around 1770. Rocking chairs were often pulled up to warm fireplaces during the long, cold New England winters. Children's rockers, with high backs and wings to ward off drafts, were used from 1790 to 1825. The heart cutout in its back was used to carry the rocker from room to room. If you collect dolls, make a half-size model of this rocker for display. Reduce all dimensions by half and lay out the pieces using a ½-inch grid.

Step 1. Study the plans carefully, checking the shape of each part. Visualize how you will make the rocking chair and what tools you will need.

Step 2. As you study the plans, note the order in which the project is to be assembled.

Step 3. Because the back, sides, and rocker have irregular shapes, they should be laid out on a 1-inch grid to make a full-size pattern on heavy paper or cardboard. Transfer the shape of each piece to the grid, and then trace it on the wood.

Step 4. Carefully cut all parts according to the materials list. Cut all parts to exact size and cut the edges exactly square (90°). Recheck all dimensions.

Step 5. Lightly sand all surfaces and edges with medium sandpaper to remove any burrs or tool marks. Keep all edges square and sharp.

Step 6. Follow the detailed illustrations and dimensions for making the parts. Check all dimensions for accuracy. Cut a smooth arc with no flat areas on the rocker. Tape the two sides together before cutting them out, so that you have an exact pair. Resand with fine-grit paper, keeping all edges sharp.

Step 7. After all the pieces have been made, dry-fit them; that is, assemble the complete project without glue or nails to check for accuracy and joint fit. If any parts fit poorly, now is the time to make corrections.

Step 8. Assemble the rocking chair, keeping everything square. Note that the rockers are not parallel; they are set at an angle.

Step 9. Finish to suit, using the general finishing instructions.

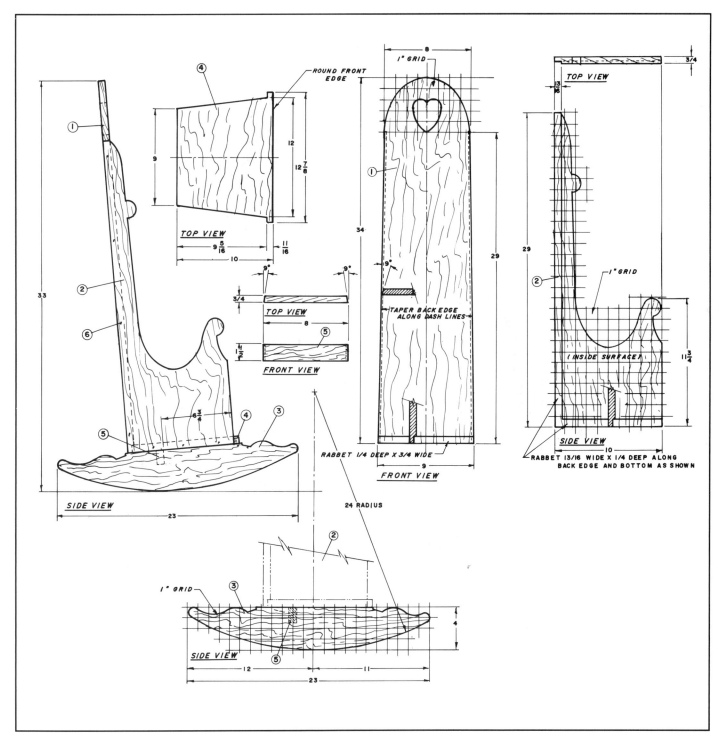

PART	INCHES	NEEDED
1 BACK	$3/4 \times 9 \times 34$	1
2 SIDES	$3/4 \times 10 \times 29$	2
3 ROCKER	$3/4 \times 4 \times 23$	2
4 SEAT	$3/4 \times 10 \times 12^{7}/_8$	1
5 BRACE	$3/4 \times 1^{1}/_2 \times 8$	1
6 SQUARE-CUT FINISH NAIL	$1^{3}/_4$	AS REQ'D

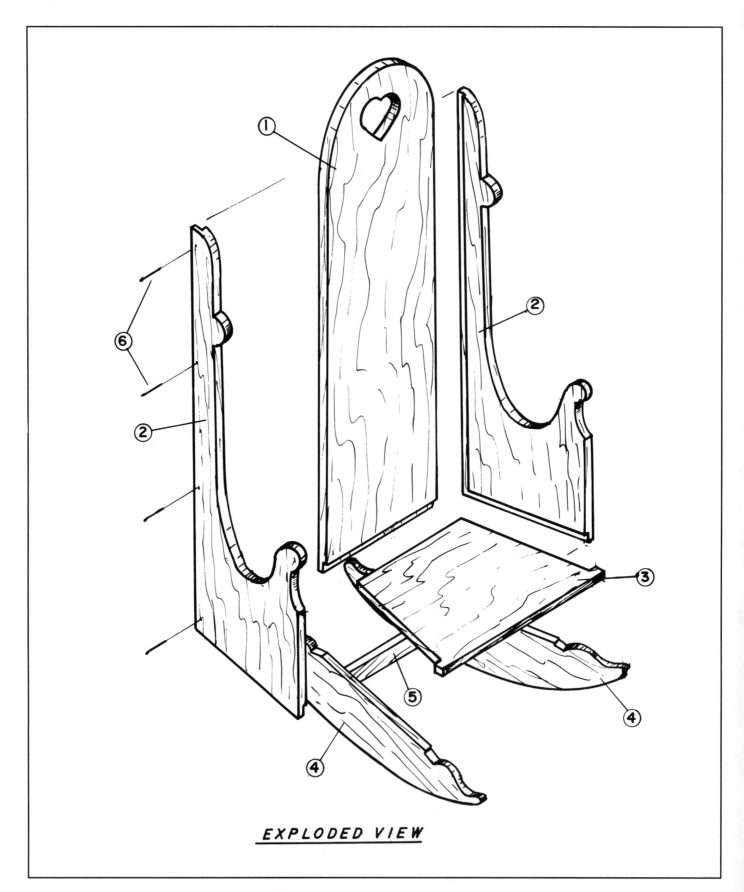

EXPLODED VIEW

Child's Sled

During the winter of 1860, Henry Morton built more than fifty sleds in his hometown of West Sumner, Maine. The demand was so great that he established a company in the nearby town of Paris. The company is still in business today.

The original sled was painted bright red with a cream pinstripe. My trick to painting pinstripes is to thin the paint slightly and use a professional, long-bristled, striping brush. These brushes are slightly expensive but well worth the price. Practice on a piece of painted scrap wood. Always pull the brush toward you as you paint the stripe and use your finger along the side of the sled as a guide. Keep a rag or cotton swab with thinner on it handy to correct mistakes. Apply a protective topcoat of varnish after the striping dries. If you don't want to try pinstriping, take your sled to a local sign shop painter who will pinstripe it in about fifteen minutes for a reasonable price.

Step 1. Study the plans carefully, checking the shape of each part. Visualize how you will make the sled and what tools you will need.

Step 2. As you study the plans, note the order in which the project is to be assembled.

Step 3. Because the runner (part 1) has an irregular shape, it should be laid out on a 1-inch grid to make a full-size pattern on heavy paper or cardboard. Transfer the shape of the piece to the grid, and then trace it on the wood. Be sure to locate the two holes for the braces (part 3).

Step 4. Carefully cut all parts according to the materials list. Cut all parts to exact size and cut the edges exactly square (90°). Recheck all dimensions.

Step 5. Lightly sand all surfaces and edges with medium sandpaper to remove any burrs or tool marks. Keep all edges square and sharp.

Step 6. Follow the detailed illustrations and dimensions for making the parts. Check all dimensions for accuracy. The two braces are made by gluing together two ¾-inch-thick pieces of wood. Resand with fine-grit paper, keeping all edges sharp.

Step 7. After all the pieces have been made, dry-fit them; that is, assemble the complete project without glue or nails to check for accuracy and joint fit. If any parts fit poorly, now is the time to make corrections.

Step 8. Assemble the sled, keeping everything square. Because oak is very hard and can split, predrill all the holes before nailing. Add the four pins (part 4) after the sled is fully assembled; these are for decoration only.

Step 9. Finish to suit, using the general finishing instructions. The sled can be left natural.

Step 10. (Optional) I made the pulls (part 5) out of an old coat hanger, but any similar material will work. Bend the steel rod to approximately the shape indicated and insert it into the runners as shown.

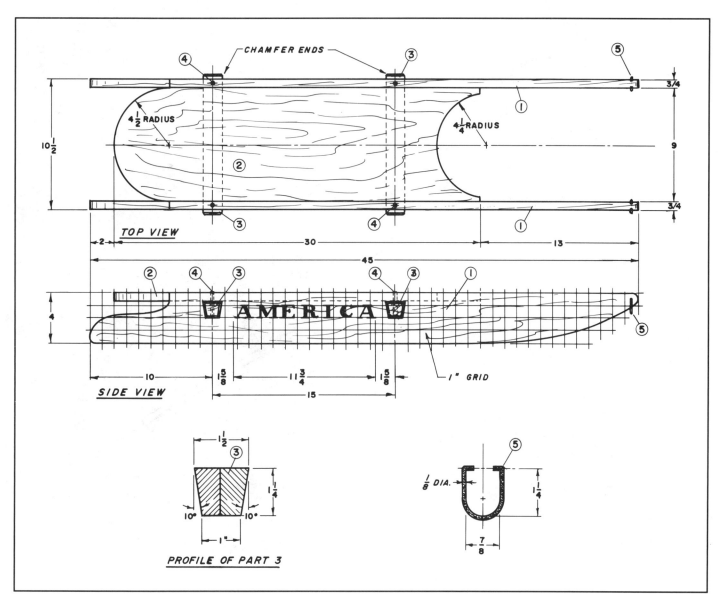

TOP VIEW

CHAMFER ENDS

$4\frac{1}{2}$ RADIUS

$4\frac{1}{4}$ RADIUS

$10\frac{1}{2}$

3/4

9

3/4

2

30

13

45

SIDE VIEW

AMERICA

1" GRID

4

10

$1\frac{5}{8}$

$11\frac{3}{4}$

$1\frac{5}{8}$

15

PROFILE OF PART 3

$1\frac{1}{2}$

$1\frac{1}{4}$

10°

10°

1"

$\frac{1}{8}$ DIA.

$1\frac{1}{4}$

$\frac{7}{8}$

PART	INCHES	NEEDED
1 RUNNER	$3/4 \times 4 \times 45$	2
2 TOP BOARD	$3/4 \times 9 \times 30$	1
3 BRACE	$1\frac{1}{4} \times 1\frac{1}{2} \times 11$	2
4 PIN	$\frac{1}{4}$ DIA. $\times 1\frac{1}{2}$	4
5 PULL	$\frac{1}{8}$ DIA. $\times 3\frac{1}{2}$	2

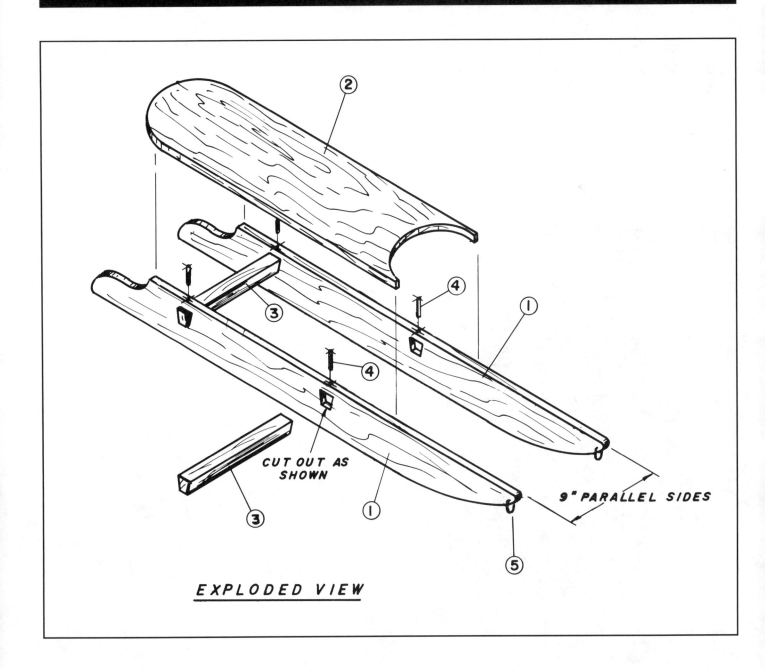

CUT OUT AS
SHOWN

9" PARALLEL SIDES

EXPLODED VIEW

Painted Bench

Benches, like footstools, come in all shapes and sizes. They were originally made to fill a specific need, and this easy-to-make bench can range in length from 36 to 60 inches to fit the spot you have picked for it. It is a rather inexpensive project and can be made from one piece of 1-inch by 12-inch pine that is 10 feet long. The bench pictured is 40 inches long. To lengthen it, lengthen the cyma curve on the skirt using a 1-inch grid. For example, if you made the vertical grid 1 inch as shown, the skirt would still be 3½ inches high. If you lengthened the horizontal grid to 1½ inches, the total length would be 60 inches. Lay out the cyma curve as you normally would to obtain the same curve extended to 60 inches.

    Step 1. Study the plans carefully, checking the shape of each part. Visualize how you will make the bench and what tools you will need.

    Step 2. As you study the plans, note the order in which the project is to be assembled.

    Step 3. Because the skirt and legs (parts 1 and 3) have irregular shapes, they should be laid out on a 1-inch grid to make a full-size pattern on heavy paper or cardboard. Transfer the shape of each piece to the grid, and then trace it on the wood.

    Step 4. Carefully cut all parts according to the materials list. Cut all parts to exact size and cut the edges exactly square (90°). Recheck all dimensions.

    Step 5. Lightly sand all surfaces and edges with medium sandpaper to remove any burrs or tool marks. Keep all edges square and sharp.

    Step 6. Follow the detailed illustrations and dimensions for making the parts. Check all dimensions for accuracy. Tape the two skirts and legs together before cutting them out so you have an exact pair. Resand with fine-grit paper, keeping all edges sharp.

Step 7. After all the pieces have been made, dry-fit them; that is, assemble the complete project without glue or nails to check for accuracy and joint fit. If any parts fit poorly, now is the time to make corrections.

Step 8. Assemble the bench, keeping everything square. Check that the project is sturdy; you wouldn't want it to come apart if someone were to stand on it.

Step 9. I recommend distressing your bench, painting it one color and repainting it another. Then sand through the top coat of paint to the first color for an old, repainted effect. See the general finishing instructions.

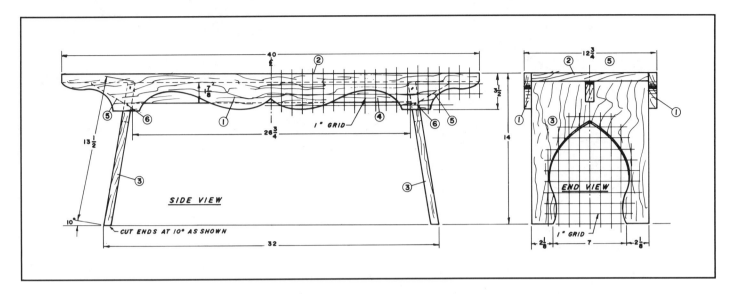

PART	INCHES	NEEDED
1 SKIRT	3/4 × 3 1/2 × 40	2
2 TOP BOARD	3/4 × 11 1/4 × 40	1
3 LEG	3/4 × 11 1/4 × 13 1/2	2
4 CENTER BRACE	3/4 × 1 7/8 × 26 3/4	1
5 END BRACE	3/4 × 1 7/8 × 3	2
6 SQUARE-CUT FINISH NAIL	2	AS REQ'D

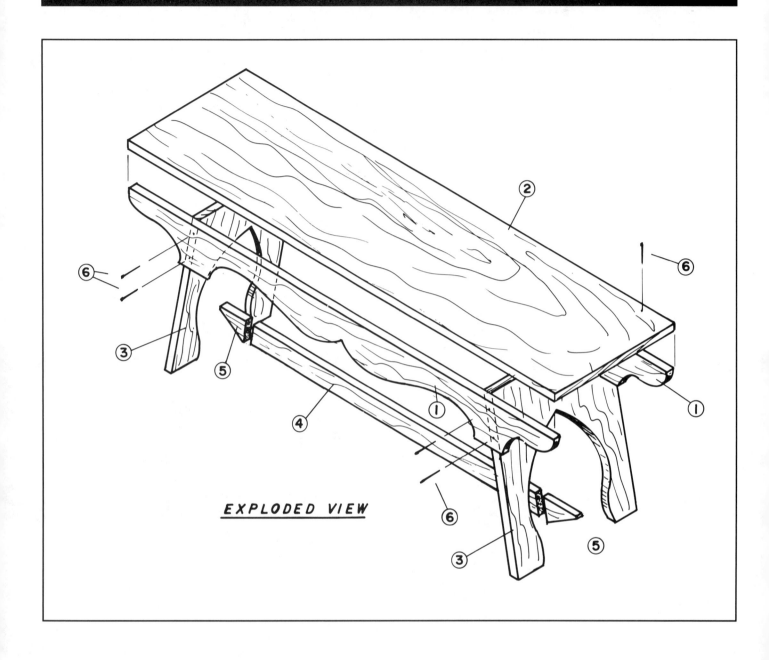

EXPLODED VIEW

Wood Box

Of all the projects I have made, I use this one the most. It surely is the handiest, since in our house in New Hampshire, we use our wood stove all winter long. Anyone who burns wood today will appreciate this project. It required only three pieces of 1-inch by 12-inch pine that are 12 feet long. The original had two leather strap hinges that were not functional or decorative, so I substituted the 35-inch brass piano hinge. The original was rather drab, so my wife, Joyce, designed the flower and leaf pattern and stenciled it.

Step 1. Study the plans carefully, checking the shape of each part. Visualize how you will make the wood box and what tools you will need.

Step 2. As you study the plans, note the order in which the project is to be assembled.

Step 3. Carefully cut all parts according to the materials list. Cut all parts to exact size and cut the edges exactly square (90°). Recheck all dimensions.

Step 4. Lightly sand all surfaces and edges with medium sandpaper to remove any burrs or tool marks. Keep all edges square and sharp.

Step 5. Follow the detailed illustrations and dimensions for making the parts. Check all dimensions for accuracy. Resand with fine-grit paper, keeping all edges sharp.

Step 6. After all the pieces have been made, dry-fit them; that is, assemble the complete project without glue or nails to check for accuracy and joint fit. If any parts fit poorly, now is the time to make corrections.

Step 7. Assemble the wood box, keeping everything square. Leave the large square-cut nails showing.

Step 8. Finish to suit, using the general finishing instructions. I painted my wood box a mustard yellow and applied a wash coat to give it an old look. As noted above, stenciling the box adds a special touch. Use the pattern shown or use another Early American stencil.

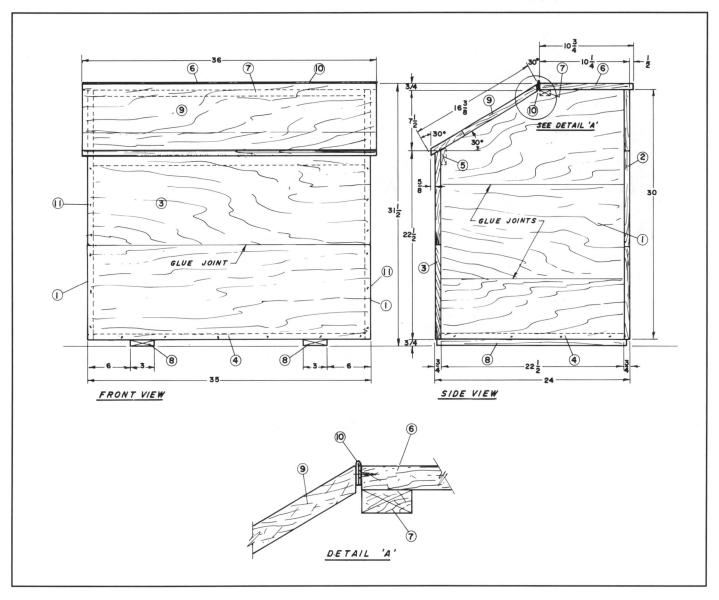

FRONT VIEW

SIDE VIEW

DETAIL 'A'

	PART	INCHES	NEEDED
1	SIDE	$3/4 \times 30 \times 22^{1}/_{2}$	2
2	BACK	$3/4 \times 30 \times 35$	1
3	FRONT	$3/4 \times 22^{1}/_{2} \times 35$	1
4	BOTTOM	$3/4 \times 22^{1}/_{2} \times 33^{1}/_{2}$	1
5	FRONT BRACE	$3/4 \times 2^{1}/_{2} \times 33^{1}/_{2}$	1
6	TOP	$3/4 \times 10^{3}/_{4} \times 36$	1
7	TOP BRACE	$3/4 \times 1^{1}/_{2} \times 33^{1}/_{2}$	1
8	FOOT	$3/4 \times 3 \times 23^{1}/_{2}$	2
9	LID	$3/4 \times 16^{3}/_{8} \times 36$	1
10	PIANO HINGE*	$5/8 \times 36$	1
11	FLOOR NAIL	8 d	AS REQ'D

*THE ORIGINAL HAD TWO LEATHER STRAP HINGES NAILED IN PLACE.

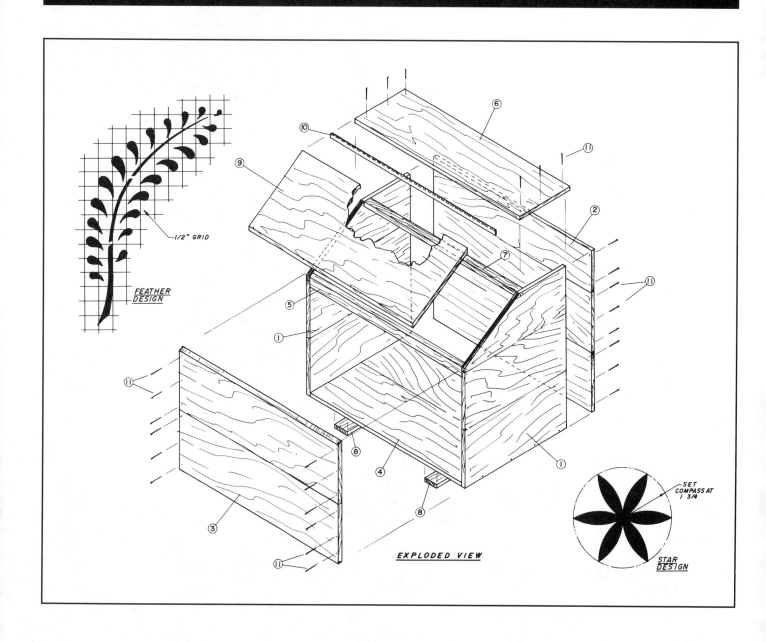

FEATHER
DESIGN

1/2" GRID

EXPLODED VIEW

SET
COMPASS AT
1 3/4

STAR
DESIGN

Silver Tray

Silver trays are as useful now as they were 150 years ago, and they add warmth and charm to any dining room setting. The original, made of walnut, turned up in an antiques shop in West Townsend, Massachusetts.

Step 1. Study the plans carefully, checking the shape of each part. Visualize how you will make the silver tray and what tools you will need.

Step 2. As you study the plans, note the order in which the project is to be assembled.

Step 3. Parts that have irregular shapes should be laid out on a ½-inch grid to make a full-size pattern on heavy paper or cardboard. Transfer the shape of each piece to the grid, and then trace it on the wood.

Step 4. Carefully cut all parts according to the materials list. Cut all parts to exact size and cut the edges exactly square (90°). Recheck all dimensions.

Step 5. Lightly sand all surfaces and edges with medium sandpaper to remove any burrs or tool marks. Keep all edges square and sharp.

Step 6. Follow the detailed illustrations and dimensions for making the parts. Check all dimensions for accuracy. Round all the edges of the center handle (part 4) before putting anything together. Make it 1/2-inch longer than noted and trim to fit at assembly. Cut the 3/8-inch-by-1/8-inch-deep dado in the two ends (part 2) as shown. Resand with fine-grit paper, keeping all edges sharp.

Step 7. After all the pieces have been made, dry-fit them; that is, assemble the complete project without glue or nails to check for accuracy and joint fit. If any parts fit poorly, now is the time to make corrections.

Step 8. Assemble the silver tray, keeping everything square.

Step 9. Finish to suit, using the general finishing instructions.

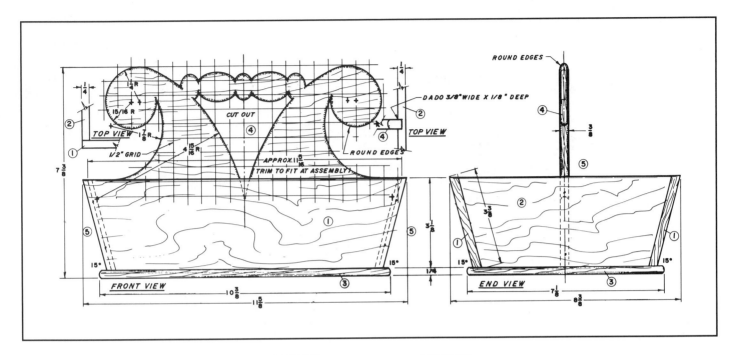

PART	INCHES	NEEDED
1 FRONT, BACK	$1/4 \times 3^3/8 \times 11^5/8$	2
2 END	$1/4 \times 3^3/8 \times 7^7/8$	2
3 BOTTOM	$1/4 \times 7^1/8 \times 10^3/8$	1
4 CENTER HANDLE	$3/8 \times 7^1/8 \times 11^5/16$	1
5 SQUARE-CUT FINISH NAIL	$3/4$	18

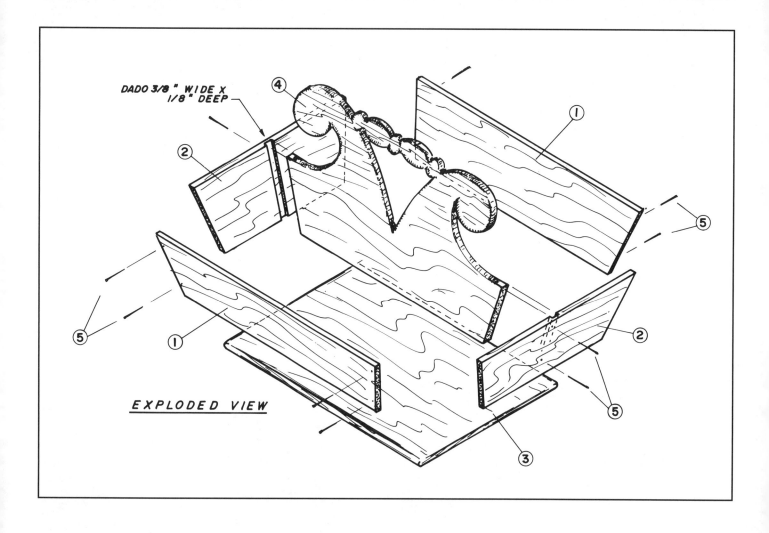

DADO 3/8" WIDE X
1/8" DEEP

EXPLODED VIEW

Yarn Winder

If you have a flax or spinning wheel, you have to have a yarn winder. This simple winder was made around 1780. To use it, wind the woven yarn around the outer pins. The pins can be adjusted in or out depending on the overall length needed.

Step 1. Study the plans carefully, checking the shape of each part. Visualize how you will make the yarn winder and what tools you will need.

Step 2. As you study the plans, note the order in which the project is to be assembled.

Step 3. Carefully cut all parts according to the materials list. Cut all parts to exact size and cut the edges exactly square (90°). Recheck all dimensions.

Step 4. Lightly sand all surfaces and edges with medium sandpaper to remove any burrs or tool marks. Keep all edges square and sharp.

Step 5. Follow the detailed illustrations and dimensions for making the parts. Check all dimensions for accuracy. You may need to glue material to make the 2³/₈-inch-thick base (part 1). Resand with fine-grit paper, keeping all edges sharp.

Step 6. After all the pieces have been made, dry-fit them; that is, assemble the complete project without glue or nails to check for accuracy and joint fit. If any parts fit poorly, now is the time to make corrections.

Step 7. Assemble the yarn winder, keeping everything square.

Step 8. Finish to suit, using the general finishing instructions.

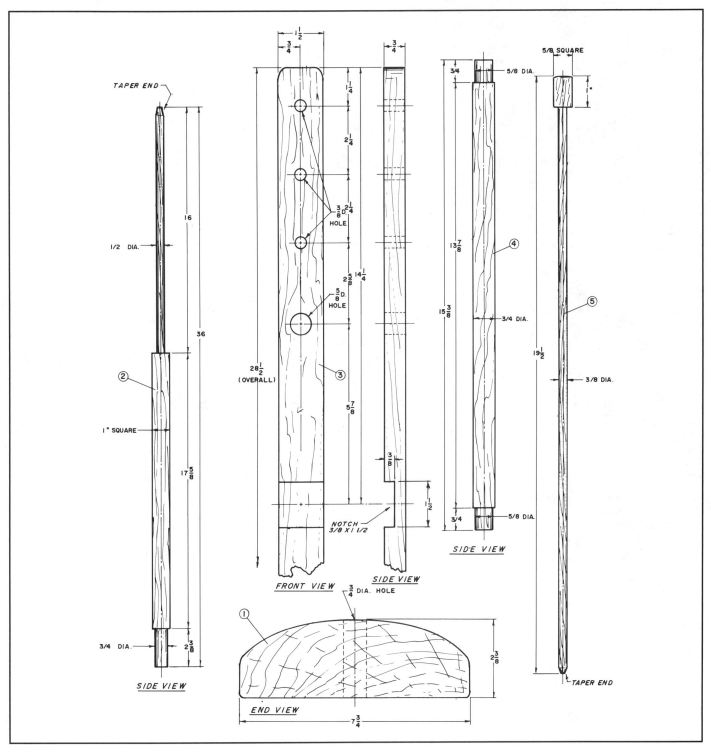

PART	INCHES	NEEDED
1 BASE	$2^3/_8 \times 7^3/_4 \times 11^1/_2$	1
2 SUPPORT POST	1 SQUARE $\times$ 36	1
3 ARM	$^3/_4 \times 1^1/_2 \times 28^1/_2$	4
4 SPACER	1 SQUARE $\times$ 15$^3/_8$	4
5 PIN	$^5/_8$ SQUARE $\times$ 19$^1/_2$	4

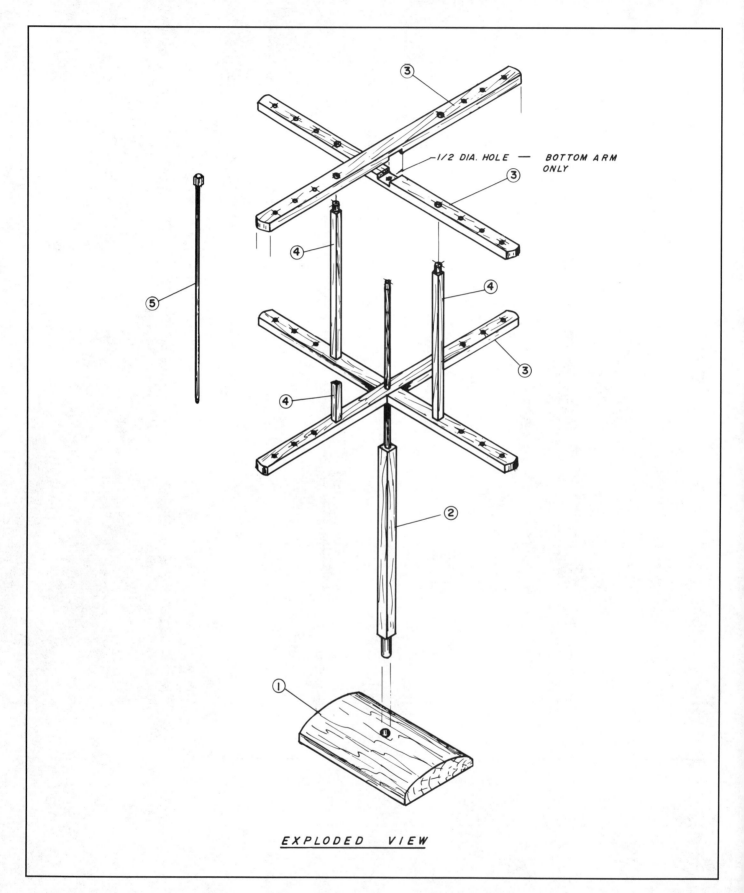

1/2 DIA. HOLE — BOTTOM ARM ONLY

EXPLODED VIEW

110

Spinning Wheel

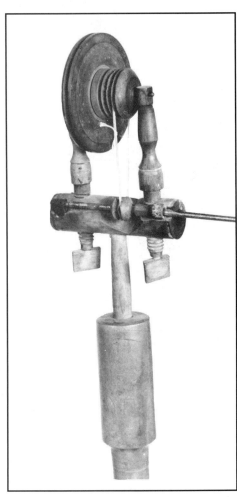

The head assembly of a spinning wheel consists of a smaller wheel, a stem, and two knobs.

Most people refer to the small, foot-operated flax wheel as a spinning wheel, which is incorrect. A spinner operated a spinning wheel by hand while standing. The large wheel turned a small spindle wheel that twisted the wool fibers into yarn. If you held the twisted wool perpendicular to the long, thin stem, the yarn would wind around the stem for temporary storage. This spinning wheel was popular around 1750 and makes a nice decorative accent today. To see one in use, visit Old Sturbridge Village in Sturbridge, Massachusetts.

Step 1. Study the plans carefully, checking the shape of each part. Visualize how you will make the spinning wheel. You will need a lathe to make the turned parts and special taps and dies to make the threads for parts 3, 7, 13, 14, and 18. If you can't find the taps and dies, you will have to carve the threads by hand.

Step 2. As you study the plans, note the order in which the project is to be assembled.

Step 3. Parts that have irregular shapes should be laid out on a grid to make a full-size pattern on heavy paper or cardboard. Transfer the shape of each piece to the grid, and then trace it on the wood.

Step 4. You may need to purchase steel for the stem (part 22) and the axle (part 12), and leather for part 20.

Step 5. Carefully cut all parts according to the materials list. Cut all parts to exact size and cut the edges exactly square (90°). Recheck all dimensions.

Step 6. Lightly sand all surfaces and edges with medium sandpaper to remove any burrs or tool marks. Keep all edges square and sharp.

Step 7. Follow the detailed illustrations and dimensions for making the parts. Check all dimensions for accuracy. Turn all parts on a lathe; make them as close as possible to the dimensioned details. The ten 5/8-inch holes are drilled at 36° intervals, as noted. Resand with fine-grit paper, keeping all edges sharp.

Step 8. After all the pieces have been made, dry-fit them; that is, assemble the complete project without glue or nails to check for accuracy and joint fit. If any parts fit poorly, now is the time to make corrections.

Step 9. Assemble the spinning wheel, keeping everything square. Depending on the wood you use, you may have to soak the 1/8-inch by 2¼-inch rim (part 8) in water so that it will bend easily. There are actually three assemblies: the base with its legs and supports; the wheel with the hub, spokes, and rim; and the head with its smaller wheel, stem, and knobs. Make each separately and put them together last. Check that everything moves freely.

Step 10. Finish to suit, using the general finishing instructions.

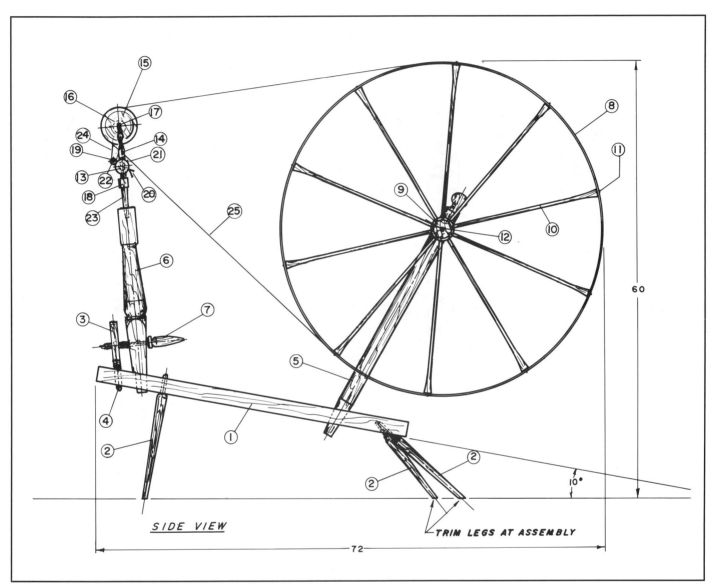

SIDE VIEW

TRIM LEGS AT ASSEMBLY

60

72

10°

	PART	INCHES	NEEDED
1	BASE	$2^1/_8 \times 5^3/_8 \times 44$	1
2	LEG	$1^3/_8$ DIA. $\times 17^1/_4$	3
3	BRACE	$1^1/_8 \times 2 \times 9^1/_2$	1
4	PIN	$^1/_8$ DIA. $\times 2$	1
5	MAIN SUPPORT	$2^3/_{16}$ DIA. $\times 38$	1
6	SUPPORT	$2^1/_2$ DIA. $\times 25^3/_8$	1
7	ADJUSTING ARM	$1^7/_{16}$ DIA. $\times 11^1/_2$	1
8	RIM	$^1/_8 \times 2^1/_4 \times 83$	2
9	HUB	$3^3/_4$ DIA. $\times 4^9/_{16}$	1
10	SPOKE	$1^1/_8$ DIA. $\times 23$	10
11	TACK	LENGTH TO SUIT	30
12	AXLE (STEEL)	$^3/_8$ DIA. $\times 7$	1
13	CENTER SUPPORT	$1^1/_2$ DIA. $\times 5^1/_2$	1

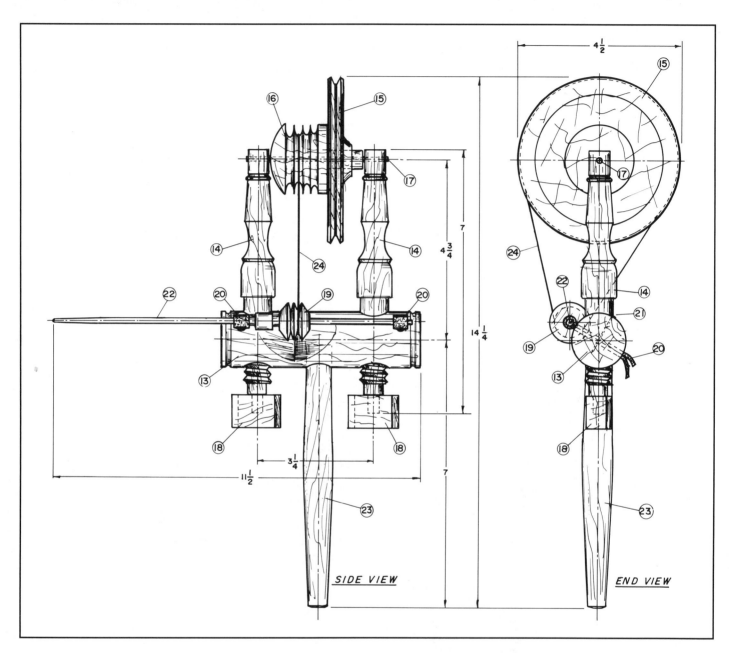

SIDE VIEW

END VIEW

PART	INCHES	NEEDED
14 STEM	$^{15}/_{16}$ DIA. × 7$^1/_{16}$	2
15 WHEEL	4$^1/_2$ DIA. × $^{11}/_{16}$	1
16 HUB	1$^7/_8$ DIA. × 2$^7/_{16}$	1
17 PIN (STEEL)	$^1/_8$ DIA. × 4	1
18 KNOB	$^1/_2$ × 1$^3/_8$ × $^7/_8$	2
19 SMALL HUB	1$^1/_{16}$ DIA. × 1$^1/_2$	1
20 SUPPORT (LEATHER)	$^1/_{16}$ × $^3/_8$ × 5	2
21 TACK		1
22 STEM	$^3/_{16}$ DIA. × 11$^1/_4$	1
23 PIN SUPPORT	$^3/_4$ DIA. × 7$^1/_4$	1
24 BELT (YARN)	LENGTH TO SUIT	1
25 DRIVE BELT	LENGTH TO SUIT	1

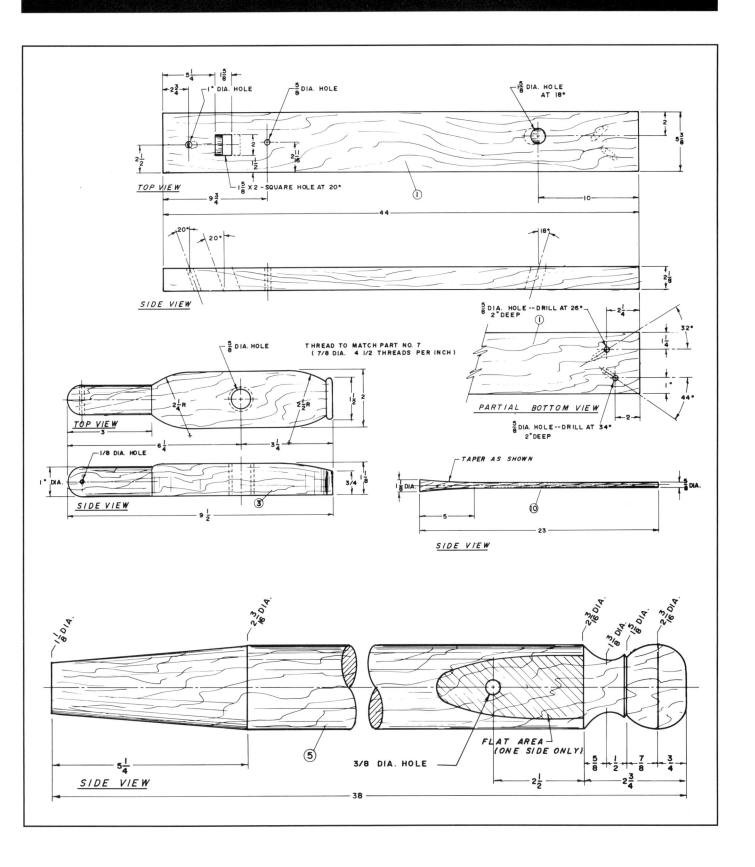

TOP VIEW

$5\frac{1}{4}$ $1\frac{5}{8}$

$2\frac{3}{4}$

1" DIA. HOLE

$\frac{5}{8}$ DIA. HOLE

$\frac{5}{8}$ DIA. HOLE AT 18°

$2\frac{1}{2}$

$2\frac{11}{16}$

2

$1\frac{1}{2}$

2

$5\frac{3}{8}$

$1\frac{5}{8}$ X 2 - SQUARE HOLE AT 20°

$9\frac{3}{4}$

44

①

10

SIDE VIEW

20°

20°

18°

$2\frac{1}{8}$

$\frac{5}{8}$ DIA. HOLE

THREAD TO MATCH PART NO. 7
($\frac{7}{8}$ DIA. 4 1/2 THREADS PER INCH)

$\frac{5}{8}$ DIA. HOLE -- DRILL AT 26°
2" DEEP

①

$2\frac{1}{4}$

32°

$1\frac{1}{4}$

TOP VIEW

$2\frac{1}{4}$R

$2\frac{1}{2}$R

$1\frac{1}{2}$

3

$6\frac{1}{4}$

$3\frac{1}{4}$

1"

44°

PARTIAL BOTTOM VIEW

1/8 DIA. HOLE

1" DIA.

$1\frac{1}{8}$

$3\frac{1}{4}$

③

$9\frac{1}{2}$

$\frac{5}{8}$ DIA. HOLE -- DRILL AT 34°
2" DEEP

2

TAPER AS SHOWN

$\frac{1}{8}$ DIA.

$\frac{5}{8}$ DIA.

5

⑩

23

SIDE VIEW

$1\frac{1}{8}$ DIA.

$2\frac{3}{16}$ DIA.

$2\frac{3}{16}$ DIA.

$3\frac{1}{8}$ DIA.

$\frac{5}{8}$ DIA.

$2\frac{3}{16}$ DIA.

FLAT AREA
(ONE SIDE ONLY)

3/8 DIA. HOLE

$5\frac{1}{4}$

⑤

$2\frac{1}{2}$

$2\frac{3}{4}$

$\frac{5}{8}$

$\frac{1}{2}$

$\frac{7}{8}$

$\frac{3}{4}$

SIDE VIEW

38

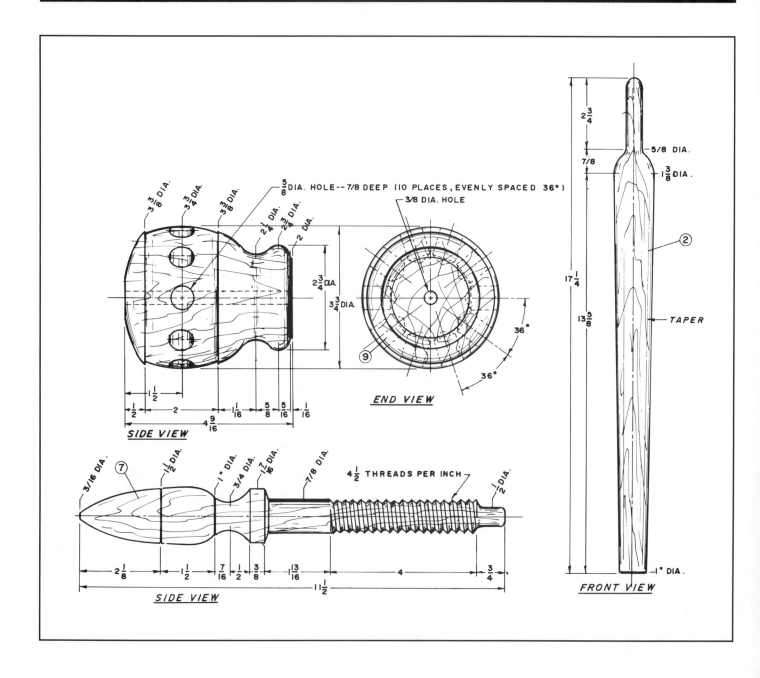

$\frac{3\frac{3}{8}}{}$ DIA. $3\frac{3}{4}$ DIA. $3\frac{3}{8}$ DIA. $2\frac{1}{4}$ DIA. $2\frac{3}{4}$ DIA.   2 DIA.

$\frac{5}{8}$ DIA. HOLE--7/8 DEEP (10 PLACES, EVENLY SPACED 36°)

3/8 DIA. HOLE

$2\frac{3}{4}$ DIA.

$3\frac{3}{4}$ DIA.

$3\frac{3}{4}$ DIA.

9

36°

36°

END VIEW

$\frac{1}{2}$ $1\frac{1}{2}$ 2 $1\frac{1}{16}$ $\frac{5}{8}$ $\frac{5}{16}$ $\frac{1}{16}$

$4\frac{9}{16}$

SIDE VIEW

3/16 DIA.   7 $1\frac{1}{2}$ DIA.   1" DIA.   3/4 DIA. $\frac{7}{16}$ DIA.   7/8 DIA. $4\frac{1}{2}$ THREADS PER INCH $\frac{1}{2}$ DIA.

$2\frac{1}{8}$ $1\frac{1}{2}$ $\frac{7}{16}$ $1\frac{1}{2}$ $\frac{3}{8}$ $1\frac{13}{16}$ 4 $\frac{3}{4}$

$11\frac{1}{2}$

SIDE VIEW

$2\frac{3}{4}$ 5/8 DIA. $1\frac{3}{8}$ DIA.   2   TAPER $17\frac{1}{4}$ $13\frac{5}{8}$ 7/8   1" DIA.

FRONT VIEW

116

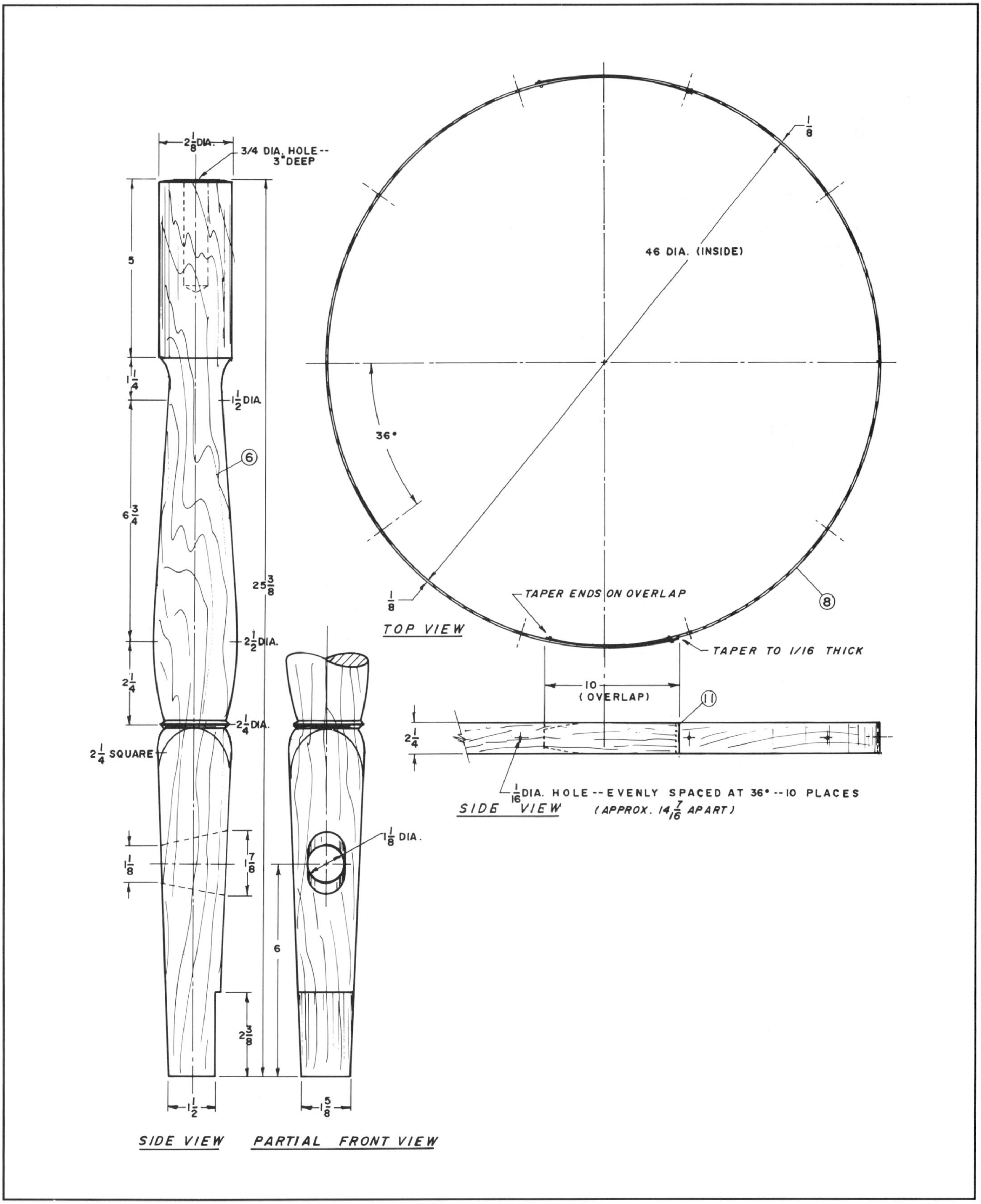
2 1/8 DIA.
3/4 DIA. HOLE -- 3" DEEP
5
1 1/4
1 1/2 DIA.
6
6 3/4
25 3/8
2 1/2 DIA.
2 1/4
2 1/4 DIA.
2 1/4 SQUARE
1 1/8
1 7/8
1 1/8 DIA.
6
2 3/8
1 1/2
1 5/8
SIDE VIEW
PARTIAL FRONT VIEW
1/8
46 DIA. (INSIDE)
36°
1/8
TAPER ENDS ON OVERLAP
8
TOP VIEW
TAPER TO 1/16 THICK
10 (OVERLAP)
11
2 1/4
1/16 DIA. HOLE -- EVENLY SPACED AT 36° -- 10 PLACES
SIDE VIEW
(APPROX. 14 7/16 APART)

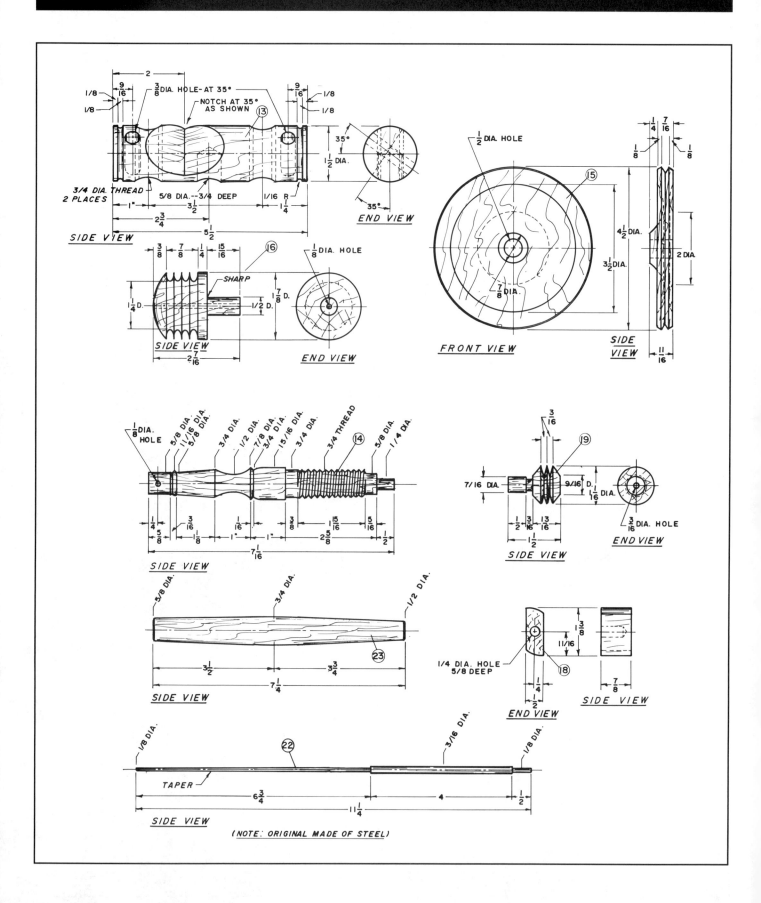

2

1/8
9/16
3/8 DIA. HOLE - AT 35°
NOTCH AT 35°
AS SHOWN
(13)
9/16
1/8
1/8
1/8

35°

1/2 DIA.

3/4 DIA. THREAD
2 PLACES

5/8 DIA.--3/4 DEEP

1/16 R
1/4

35°

END VIEW

1"
3 1/2
2 3/4
5 1/2

SIDE VIEW

3/8
7/8
1/4
15/16
(16)

SHARP

1/8 DIA. HOLE

1 1/4 D.

1/2 D.

1 7/8 D.

SIDE VIEW
2 7/16

END VIEW

1/2 DIA. HOLE

(15)

4 1/2 DIA.

3 1/2 DIA.

7/8 DIA.

FRONT VIEW

1/4
7/16
1/8
1/8

2 DIA.

SIDE
VIEW

11/16

1/8 DIA.
HOLE
5/8 DIA.
11/16 DIA.
5/8 DIA.
3/4 DIA.
1/2 DIA.
7/8 DIA.
3/4 DIA.
15/16 DIA.
3/4 DIA.
3/4 THREAD
(14)
5/8 DIA.
1/4 DIA.

1/4
5/8
3/16
1 1/8
1/16
1"
3/4
3/8
15/16
2 5/8
5/8
1/2
7 1/16

SIDE VIEW

3/16
(19)
7/16 DIA.
9/16 D.
1 1/8 DIA.
3/16 DIA. HOLE

1/2
3/16
13/16
1/2

SIDE VIEW

END VIEW

5/8 DIA.
3/4 DIA.
1/2 DIA.
(23)

3 1/2
3 3/4
7 1/4

SIDE VIEW

3/8
11/16
1/4 DIA. HOLE
5/8 DEEP
(18)

1/4

END VIEW

7/8

SIDE VIEW

1/8 DIA.
(22)
3/16 DIA.
1/8 DIA.

TAPER

6 3/4
4
1/2
11 1/4

SIDE VIEW

(NOTE: ORIGINAL MADE OF STEEL)

118

Apothecary Chest

In Colonial America, apothecary chests were used to store drugs, herbs, and kitchen or bath supplies. An interesting feature of this chest is the unique series of saw kerfs that make a design in the drawer fronts. This chest is a great place to store or hide small things that usually clutter the house. The drawers are just boxes without lids; the lips, however, are only on the sides and tops. The trick to making drawers is to use cutting jigs so that all matching pieces are exactly the same shape and size.

   Step 1. Study the plans carefully, checking the shape of each part. Visualize how you will make the apothecary chest and what tools you will need.

   Step 2. As you study the plans, note the order in which the project is to be assembled.

   Step 3. Carefully cut all parts according to the materials list. Cut all parts to exact size and cut the edges exactly square (90°). Recheck all dimensions.

Step 4. Lightly sand all surfaces and edges with medium sandpaper to remove any burrs or tool marks. Keep all edges square and sharp.

Step 5. Follow the detailed illustrations and dimensions for making the parts. Check all dimensions for accuracy. If you do not have the exact router bits for the moldings, purchase special cutters or buy similar moldings. The saw cuts in the drawer fronts (part 10) should be made with a $1/16$-inch saw blade. A small Dremel table saw makes the perfect cut for this project. Resand with fine-grit paper, keeping all edges sharp.

Step 6. After all the pieces have been made, dry-fit them; that is, assemble the complete project without glue or nails to check for accuracy and joint fit. If any parts fit poorly, now is the time to make corrections. Cut all moldings to fit at 45°. If you used saw stops and all drawer parts are exactly the same, all twelve drawers should be interchangeable.

Step 7. Assemble the apothecary chest, keeping everything square.

Step 8. Finish to suit, using the general finishing instructions.

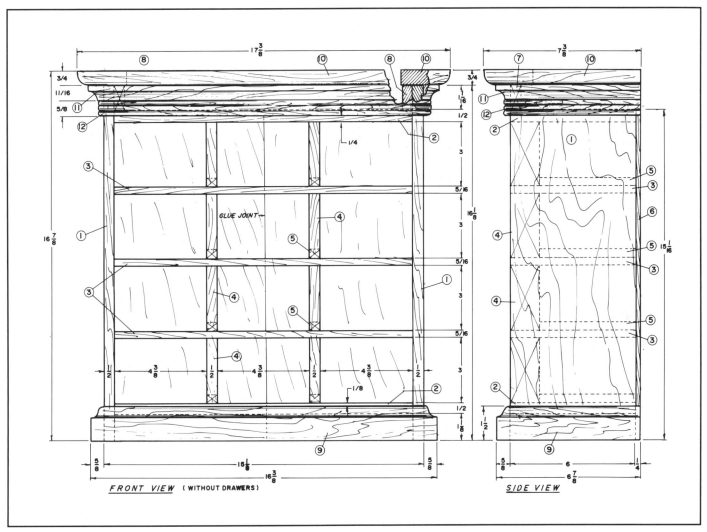

FRONT VIEW (WITHOUT DRAWERS)   SIDE VIEW

	PART	INCHES	NEEDED
1	SIDE	$1/2 \times 6 \times 16 1/8$	2
2	TOP, BOTTOM	$1/2 \times 6 \times 14 1/8$	2
3	RAIL	$5/16 \times 6 \times 14 1/8$	3
4	DIVIDER	$1/2 \times 1 1/2 \times 3$	8
5	GUIDE	$3/8 \times 1/2 \times 4 1/2$	8
6	BACK	$1/4 \times 15 1/8 \times 15 1/16$	1
7	FRONT BRACE	$1/2 \times 1 1/16 \times 14 1/8$	1
8	SIDE BRACE	$1/2 \times 1 1/16 \times 5 3/4$	2
9	BASE MOLDING	$5/8 \times 1 1/2 \times 36$	1
10	TOP TRIM	$3/4 \times 2 1/4 \times 36$	1
11	CENTER MOLDING	$5/8 \times 11/16 \times 36$	1
12	BOTTOM MOLDING	$1/4 \times 5/8 \times 36$	1
13	DRAWER FRONT	$1/2 \times 3 1/8 \times 4 5/8$	12
14	DRAWER SIDE	$1/4 \times 2 15/16 \times 5 7/8$	24
15	DRAWER BACK	$1/4 \times 2 11/16 \times 3 13/16$	12
16	DRAWER BOTTOM	$1/4 \times 3 15/16 \times 5 3/4$	12
17	BRAD	$5/8$	AS REQ'D
18	WHITE GLASS PULL	$5/8$ DIA.	12

121

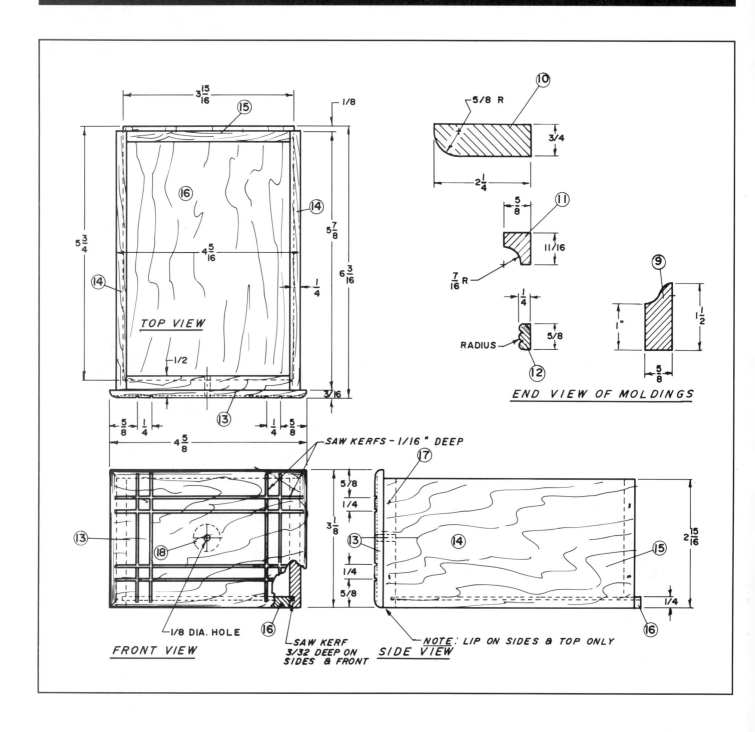

TOP VIEW

FRONT VIEW

SIDE VIEW

END VIEW OF MOLDINGS

SAW KERFS-1/16" DEEP

1/8 DIA. HOLE

SAW KERF 3/32 DEEP ON SIDES & FRONT

NOTE: LIP ON SIDES & TOP ONLY

RADIUS

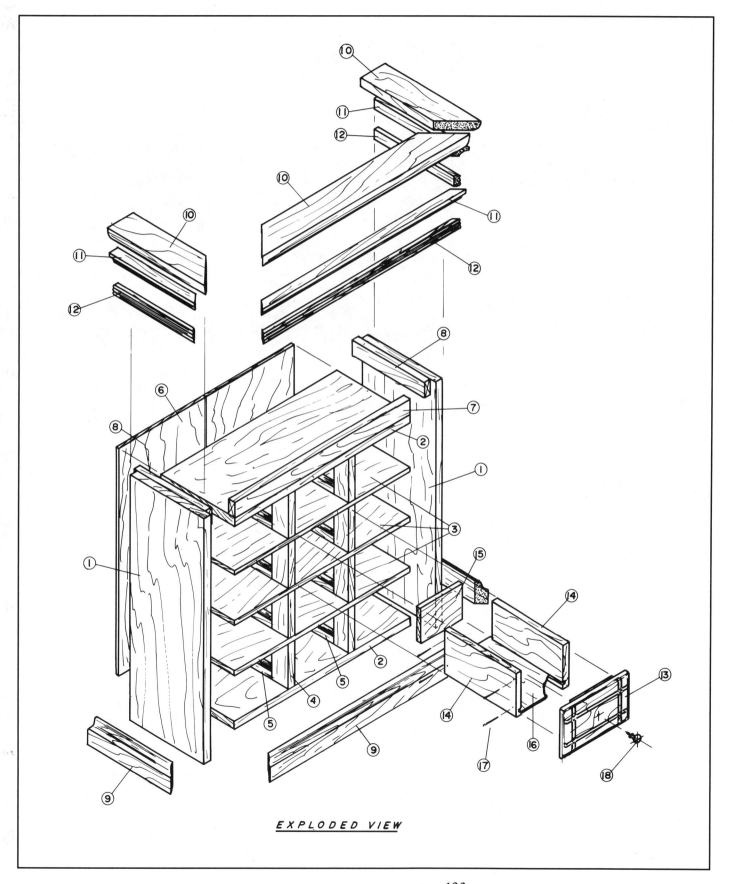

Dough Box with Legs

Years ago most housewives wanted the luxury of a dough box (or dough boy), especially if they baked a lot of bread. The splayed-leg original dough box shown was especially envied. Dough was mixed and kneaded on the surface, and then allowed to rise inside the box. This model, with its beautiful dovetail construction, was used from 1750 to 1840 or so. Today the dough box is great for storage; we use ours for those old magazines we just can't seem to part with. The top surface is a lovely display spot for your original antiques or as an extra side table.

Step 1. Study the plans carefully, checking the shape of each part. Visualize how you will make the dough box and what tools you will need.

Step 2. As you study the plans, note the order in which the project is to be assembled.

Step 3. After turning the legs on a lathe, cut the ³⁄₈-inch by ³⁄₄-inch mortise 5¼ inches long as illustrated. The top surface is cut at 9°.

Step 4. Carefully cut all parts according to the materials list. Cut all parts to exact size and cut the edges exactly square (90°). Recheck all dimensions.

Step 5. Lightly sand all surfaces and edges with medium sandpaper to remove any burrs or tool marks. Keep all edges square and sharp.

Step 6. Follow the detailed illustrations and dimensions for making the parts. Check all dimensions for accuracy. The dovetails are not difficult—be sure to take care when laying them out. They must be cut at an odd angle to get the 15° slant on the front and back surfaces. Don't forget to cut the top and bottom edges of the end and sides (parts 6 and 7) at 15° as shown. Resand with fine-grit paper, keeping all edges sharp.

Step 7. After all the pieces have been made, dry-fit them; that is, assemble the complete project without glue or nails to check for accuracy and joint fit. If any parts fit poorly, now is the time to make corrections.

Step 8. Assemble the dough box, keeping everything square. There are really three assemblies: the base assembly with legs and divider, the dovetailed top area with the sides and ends, and the top with batten boards. Make each separately and put them together last. The top assembly is not fastened; rather, it just sits on top.

Step 9. Finish to suit, using the general finishing instructions.

Pattern begins on next page.

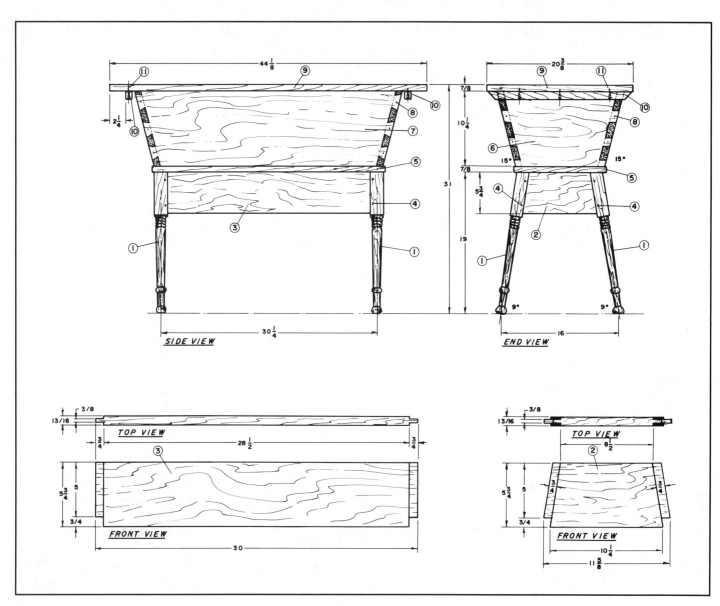

PART	INCHES	NEEDED
1 LEG	1³/₄ SQ. × 19¹/₂	4
2 END SKIRT	¹³/₁₆ × 5³/₄ × 11⁵/₈	2
3 FRONT, BACK SKIRT	¹³/₁₆ × 5³/₄ × 30	2
4 PEG	³/₁₆ DIA. × 1¹/₂	16
5 DIVIDER	⁷/₈ × 12³/₈ × 30¹/₈	1
6 END	¹³/₁₆ × 10³/₄ × 17¹/₂	2
7 SIDE	¹³/₁₆ × 10³/₄ × 37¹/₄	2
8 SQUARE-CUT FINISH NAIL	1³/₄	AS REQ'D
9 TOP	⁷/₈ × 20³/₈ × 44¹/₈	1
10 BATTEN	⁷/₈ × 1 × 20¹/₄	2
11 FLAT-HEAD SCREW	NO. 8—1¹/₂	6

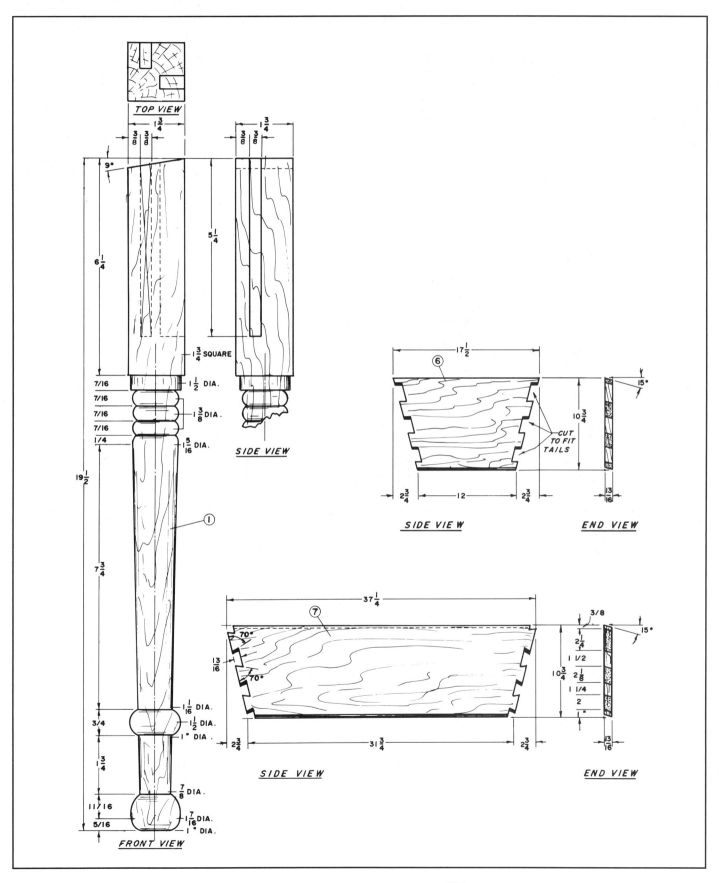

TOP VIEW

$1\frac{3}{4}$

$\frac{3}{8}$ $\frac{3}{8}$

9°

$1\frac{3}{4}$

$\frac{3}{8}$ $\frac{3}{8}$

$6\frac{1}{4}$

$5\frac{1}{4}$

$1\frac{3}{4}$ SQUARE

7/16 — $1\frac{1}{2}$ DIA.
7/16
7/16 — $1\frac{3}{8}$ DIA.
7/16
1/4 — $1\frac{5}{16}$ DIA.

$19\frac{1}{2}$

SIDE VIEW

①

$7\frac{3}{4}$

$1\frac{1}{16}$ DIA.
3/4 — $1\frac{1}{2}$ DIA.
1" DIA.

$1\frac{3}{4}$

7/8 DIA.
11/16 — $1\frac{7}{16}$ DIA.
5/16 — 1" DIA.

FRONT VIEW

⑥

$17\frac{1}{2}$

15°

$10\frac{3}{4}$

CUT TO FIT TAILS

$2\frac{3}{4}$ 12 $2\frac{3}{4}$

$\frac{13}{16}$

SIDE VIEW   END VIEW

⑦

$37\frac{1}{4}$

3/8

70°

$\frac{13}{16}$

70°

$2\frac{1}{4}$

$1\frac{1}{2}$

$10\frac{3}{4}$ $2\frac{1}{8}$

$1\frac{1}{4}$

2
1"

15°

$2\frac{3}{4}$ $31\frac{3}{4}$ $2\frac{3}{4}$

$\frac{13}{16}$

SIDE VIEW   END VIEW

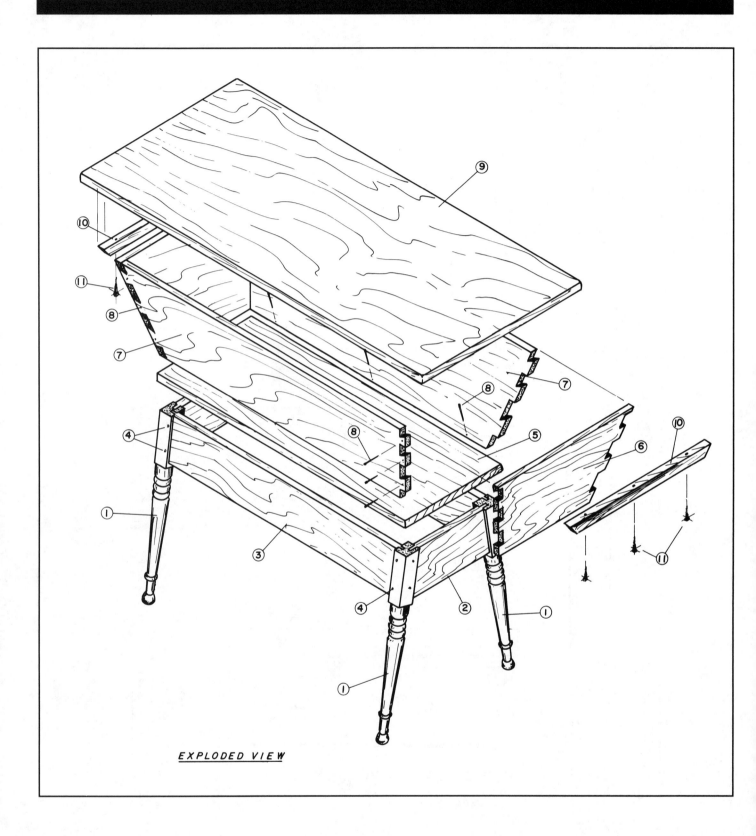

EXPLODED VIEW

128

Chippendale Mirror

Since I found that full-size Chippendale-style mirrors sell for $225 to $350 at local furniture store, I did some research and came up with this copy of an early Chippendale mirror.

The official Chippendale period, 1750 to 1785, was attributed to Thomas Chippendale of London. In 1754 he published *The Gentleman and Cabinet Maker's Directory*, the most complete, comprehensive manual at the time. His book provided inspiration for craftsmen in the American colonies and around the world. As a result, Thomas Chippendale is credited with the furniture designs of that era.

129

A mirror like this should be made of mahogany, cherry, walnut, or maple (preferably curly maple). I have included two mirror sizes in the plans. The original is very large, perhaps too big for most of today's homes. Use the smaller dimensions if you think the original size is too large for your house.

Step 1. Study the plans carefully, checking the shape of each part. Visualize how you will make the mirror and what tools you will need.

Step 2. As you study the plans, note the order in which the project is to be assembled.

Step 3. The sides, top, and bottom (parts 1 and 2) can be made using a combination of router or shaper bits, but for an exact profile, use a router bit with a ½-inch shank diameter manufactured by Cascade Tools (see the list of suppliers). The company will make a special bit of the required shape according to the drawings. This bit can be used to construct many other mirrors and picture frames, so the investment is well worth the cost.

Step 4. Carefully cut all parts to overall size according to the materials list. Sand all surfaces well to reduce the amount of finish sanding you have to do later.

Step 5. Cut the profile shape of the molding face (parts 1 and 2). Make a few extra pieces in case of error. Cut out the rabbet as shown.

Step 6. Make exact 45° cuts at the ends, taking care to hold the exact lengths. Make the ⅛-inch-wide by ¼-inch-deep grooves in the 45° cut for the splines (part 3). It is important to note the direction of the grain in part 3.

Step 7. Glue the frame together using parts 1, 2, and 3. Keep all corners at exactly 90°. After the glue sets, cut the groove along the top and bottom edges as shown; cut the groove down from the top and up from the bottom as noted on the plans for the scroll pieces (parts 4, 5, 6, and 7).

Step 8. Transfer the full-size patterns of the scrolls to the wood. Before cutting them out, check that the distance from X to Y (see top and bottom of scroll pattern layouts) is exactly the same as the outside width of the frame you made. Adjust your pattern if necessary. Carefully cut out the top and bottom scroll (parts 4 and 5).

Step 9. Tape together the two pieces of wood for the top side scroll (part 6) and the two pieces for the bottom side scroll (part 7). Transfer the patterns to the top pieces and cut them out as a pair. If necessary, sand them as a pair as well.

Step 10. Glue the scrolls to the frame assembly. Check for tight fit at the four 45° joints.

Step 11. After the glue sets, add the brace (part 8) and the four blocks (part 9). Resand using very fine sandpaper.

Step 12. Cut the backboard (part 11) to size. Taper all four edges at 10° or so; leave about ⅛ inch on all four edges as shown.

Step 13. Purchase the mirror. Have it cut to size after you finish the project to ensure a loose fit; it is necessary to allow for expansion of the wood.

Step 14. Finish to suit, using the general finishing instructions.

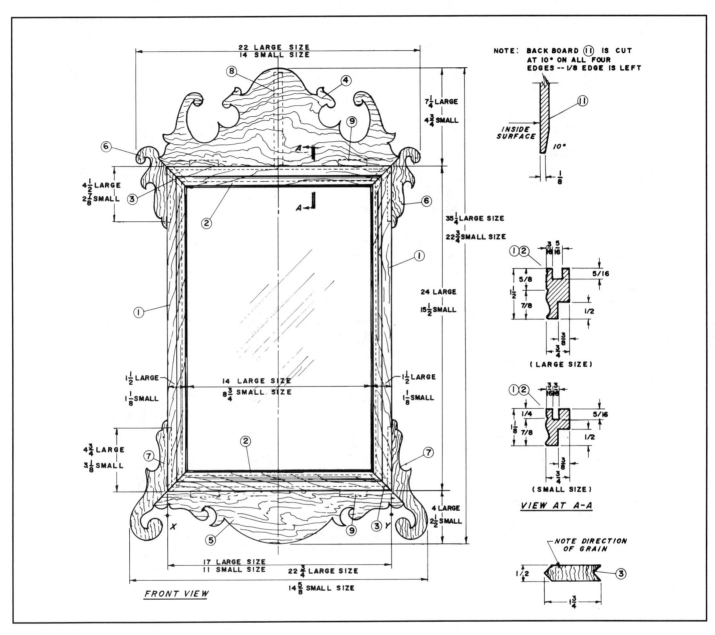

FRONT VIEW

PART		INCHES (LARGE)	INCHES (SMALL)	NEEDED
1	SIDE	$3/4 \times 1\frac{1}{2} \times 24$	$3/4 \times 1\frac{1}{8} \times 15\frac{1}{2}$	2
2	TOP, BOTTOM	$3/4 \times 1\frac{1}{2} \times 17$	$3/4 \times 1\frac{1}{8} \times 11$	2
3	SPLINE	$1/8 \times 1/2 \times 1\frac{3}{4}$	$1/8 \times 1/2 \times 1\frac{1}{4}$	4
4	TOP SCROLL	$5/16 \times 7\frac{5}{8} \times 18\frac{1}{2}$	$3/16 \times 5 \times 12$	1
5	BOTTOM SCROLL	$5/16 \times 4\frac{1}{4} \times 19\frac{1}{4}$	$3/16 \times 2\frac{3}{4} \times 12\frac{3}{8}$	1
6	TOP, SIDE SCROLL	$5/16 \times 2\frac{3}{4} \times 6\frac{5}{16}$	$3/16 \times 1\frac{3}{4} \times 4\frac{1}{8}$	2
7	BOTTOM, SIDE SCROLL	$5/16 \times 3\frac{1}{4} \times 9$	$3/16 \times 2\frac{3}{16} \times 5\frac{3}{4}$	2
8	CENTER BRACE	$1/4 \times 5/8 \times 7$	$1/4 \times 1/2 \times 4\frac{1}{2}$	1
9	BLOCK	$1/4 \times 1/2 \times 1\frac{1}{2}$	$1/4 \times 1/2 \times 1\frac{1}{2}$	4
10	MIRROR	$3/32 \times 14\frac{7}{8} \times 21\frac{7}{8}$	$3/32 \times 9\frac{5}{8} \times 14\frac{1}{8}$	1
11	BACKBOARD	$5/16 \times 14\frac{7}{8} \times 21\frac{7}{8}$	$5/16 \times 9\frac{5}{8} \times 14\frac{1}{8}$	1
12	SQUARE-CUT FINISH NAIL	$3/4$	$3/4$	8

131

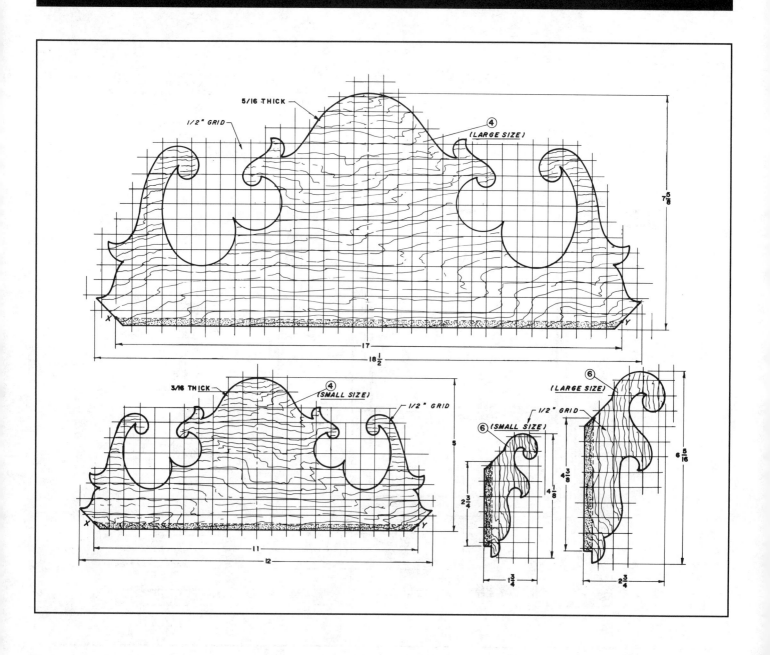

5/16 THICK

1/2" GRID

④ (LARGE SIZE)

7 5/8

17

18 1/2

3/16 THICK

④ (SMALL SIZE)

1/2" GRID

X   Y

11

12

5

⑥ (LARGE SIZE)

1/2" GRID

⑥ (SMALL SIZE)

6 5/16

4 3/8

4 1/8

2 3/4

1 3/4

2 3/4

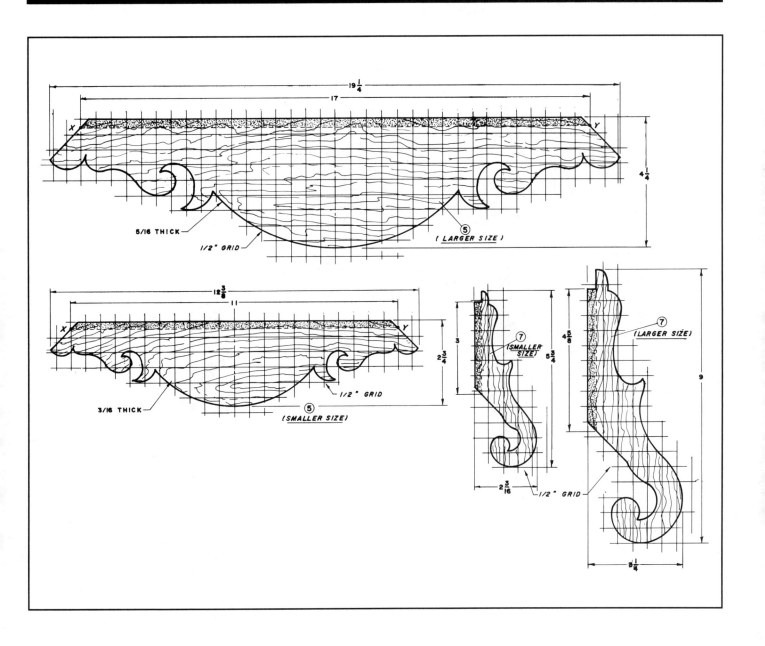

19¼
17
X   Y
4¼
5/16 THICK
1/2" GRID
⑤
(LARGER SIZE)

12⅜
11
X   Y
2¾
3/16 THICK
1/2" GRID
⑤
(SMALLER SIZE)

3
⑦
(SMALLER SIZE)
2³⁄₁₆
1/2" GRID

4⅝
⑦
(LARGER SIZE)
5¾
9
3¼

133

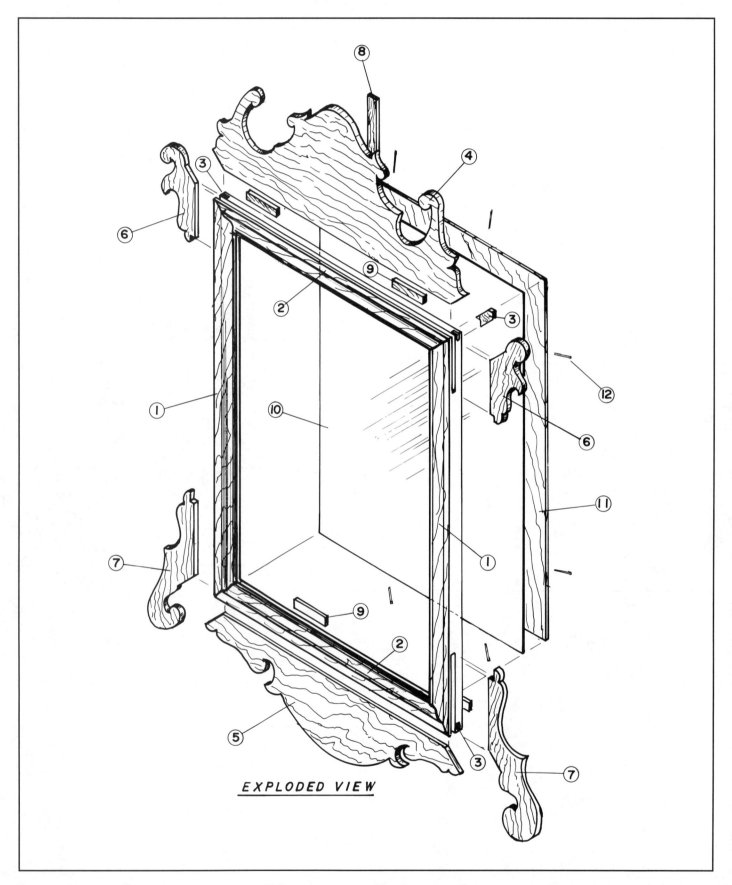

EXPLODED VIEW

Hunt Table

The pine original of this waist-high hunt table was found in North Carolina. The hunt table, also called a sofa table, was used for cooking,
serving, and eating. Today it makes a great entrance or hall table. It is
quite popular in my family; my daughter Julie wants it for her hall, but my
daughter Joy wants it for a living room divider. Unfortunately, I made only
one table. If the table seems too high to you, make the legs 2 or 3 inches
shorter than illustrated.

Step 1. Study the plans carefully, checking the shape of each part.
Visualize how you will make the table and what tools you will need.

Step 2. As you study the plans, note the order in which the project
is to be assembled.

Step 3. Because the front trim (part 5) has an irregular shape, it
should be laid out on a 1-inch grid to make a full-size pattern on heavy
paper or cardboard. Transfer the shape of each piece to the grid, and then
trace it on the wood.

Step 4. Carefully cut all parts according to the materials list. Cut all parts to exact size and cut the edges exactly square (90°). Recheck all dimensions.

Step 5. Lightly sand all surfaces and edges with medium sandpaper to remove any burrs or tool marks. Keep all edges square and sharp.

Step 6. Follow the detailed illustrations and dimensions for making the parts. Check all dimensions for accuracy. If you have a table saw taper jig, use it to cut the taper on the legs. Note that the taper on the legs is cut on the "inner" surfaces only (refer to the plans). Cut the 1/4-inch-wide by 11/16-inch-deep mortise in the legs (part 1) 6½ inches long. Cut the ¾-inch-wide by 3½-inch-long mortise in the back (part 4) to accept the tenon of the divider (part 10). Resand with fine-grit paper, keeping all edges sharp.

Step 7. Make the two drawers according to the illustration. Check that they fit into the openings with a low clearance.

Step 8. After all the pieces have been made, dry-fit them; that is, assemble the complete project without glue or nails to check for accuracy and joint fit. If any parts fit poorly, now is the time to make corrections.

Step 9. Assemble the table, keeping everything square.

Step 10. Finish to suit, using the general finishing instructions.

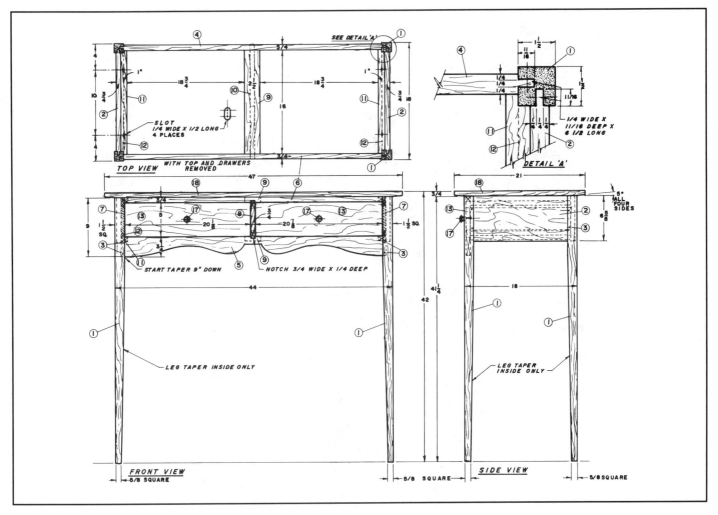

PART		INCHES	NEEDED
1	LEG	$1^{1}/_{2} \times 1^{1}/_{2} \times 41^{1}/_{4}$	4
2	END	$^{3}/_{4} \times 6^{5}/_{8} \times 16^{3}/_{8}$	2
3	PIN	$^{1}/_{4}$ DIA. $\times 1^{1}/_{2}$	14
4	BACK	$^{3}/_{4} \times 6^{5}/_{8} \times 42^{3}/_{8}$	1
5	FRONT TRIM	$^{3}/_{4} \times 3^{1}/_{4} \times 42^{3}/_{8}$	1
6	FRONT TOP	$^{3}/_{4} \times ^{3}/_{4} \times 42^{3}/_{8}$	1
7	SPACER	$^{1}/_{4} \times ^{11}/_{16} \times 5$	2
8	VERTICAL BAR	$^{3}/_{4} \times ^{3}/_{4} \times 5^{1}/_{2}$	1
9	STRETCHER CENTER	$^{3}/_{4} \times 2^{1}/_{2} \times 16$	2
10	DIVIDER	$^{3}/_{4} \times 5^{1}/_{2} \times 16^{3}/_{4}$	1
11	STRETCHER END	$^{3}/_{4} \times 1 \times 16$	4
12	GUIDE	$^{3}/_{4} \times ^{3}/_{4} \times 15$	4
13	DRAWER FRONT	$^{3}/_{4} \times 4^{15}/_{16} \times 20^{1}/_{16}$	2
14	DRAWER SIDE	$^{3}/_{8} \times 4^{15}/_{16} \times 17^{3}/_{8}$	4
15	DRAWER BACK	$^{3}/_{8} \times 4^{15}/_{16} \times 19^{11}/_{16}$	2
16	DRAWER BOTTOM	$^{1}/_{4} \times 16^{3}/_{4} \times 19^{11}/_{16}$	2
17	DRAWER PULL (BRASS)	$^{3}/_{4}$ DIA.	2
18	TOP	$^{3}/_{4} \times 21 \times 47$	1
19	ROUND-HEAD SCREW	NO. $8 \times 1^{3}/_{8}$	4

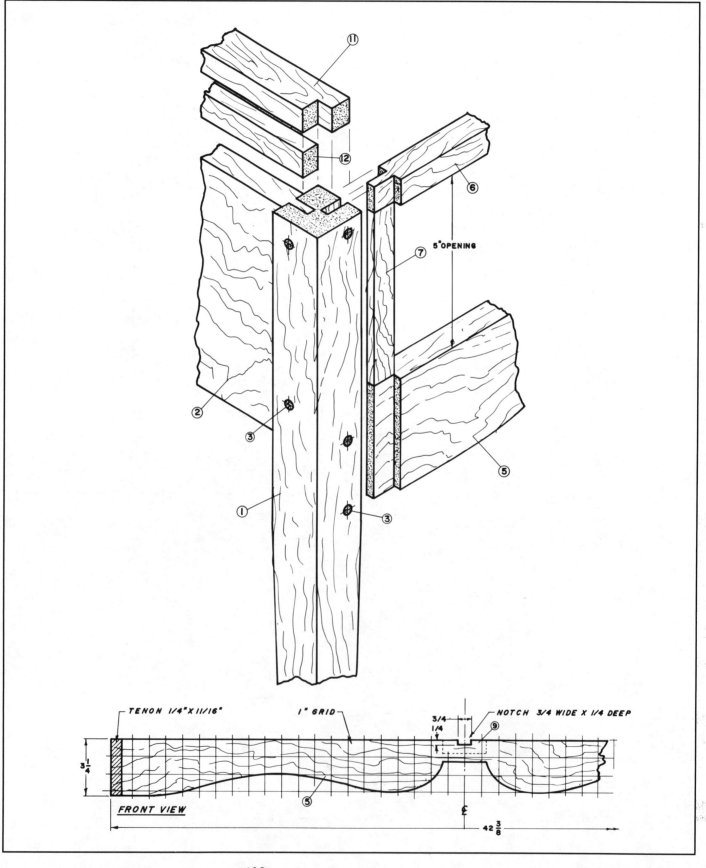

5"OPENING

TENON 1/4"X 11/16"   1" GRID   NOTCH 3/4 WIDE X 1/4 DEEP

3/4
1/4

3 1/4

FRONT VIEW

42 3/8

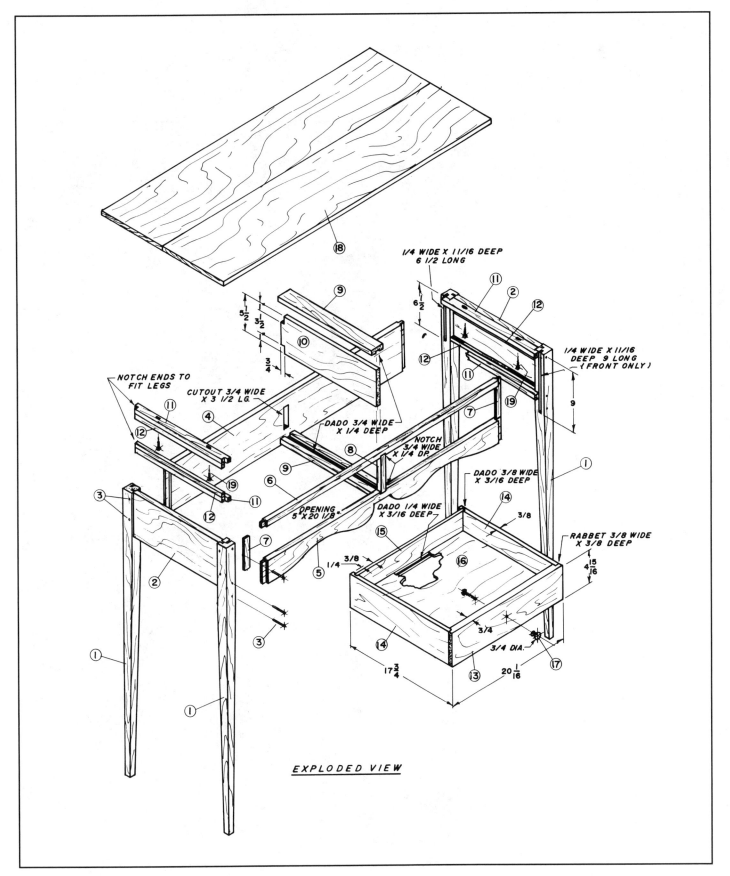

1/4 WIDE X 11/16 DEEP
6 1/2 LONG

⑪
②
⑫

6½

⑫
⑪
⑨

1/4 WIDE X 11/16
DEEP 9 LONG
(FRONT ONLY)

⑲

⑨

5½   3½

⑩

3/4

NOTCH ENDS TO
FIT LEGS

CUTOUT 3/4 WIDE
X 3 1/2 LG.

④

⑪
⑫

DADO 3/4 WIDE
X 1/4 DEEP

⑦

⑧

NOTCH
3/4 WIDE
X 1/4 DP.

9

DADO 3/8 WIDE
X 3/16 DEEP

①

⑲

⑨

⑥

⑪
⑫

OPENING
5 X 20 1/8

DADO 1/4 WIDE
X 3/16 DEEP

⑮

⑭

3/8

RABBET 3/8 WIDE
X 3/8 DEEP

③

⑦

⑯

⑤

1/4   3/8

4 15/16

②

①

③

③

⑭

3/4

3/4 DIA.

⑰

⑬

17 3/4

20 1/16

①

①

EXPLODED VIEW

139

Early Open Hutch

As pewter and pottery began to replace wooden plates, the open hutch became popular. At first, nails were used to hold the plates vertically; eventually, grooves replaced nails. These hutches usually had two or three open shelves at the top to display the pewter and pottery plates and a closed cupboard underneath with one or two shelves to store kitchen utensils. Open hutches gave way to the more formal china cabinets of the 1800s as low-priced pressed-glass plates replaced pewter and pottery.

I found this open hutch in Peterborough, New Hampshire. Although I like it, especially the fishtail pattern of the legs or skirt, I think the bottom section is too wide. Each side of the original and the copy, 20¾ inches wide, was made from one very wide board. If you can't find wood that thick, glue pieces together for the extra width. This project is not very difficult; it is just like making a wall box.

Step 1. Study the plans carefully, checking the shape of each part. Visualize how you will make the open hutch and what tools you will need.

Step 2. As you study the plans, note the order in which the project is to be assembled.

Step 3. Since the leg detail and the sides (part 1) have irregular shapes, they should be laid out on a ½-inch grid to make a full-size pattern on heavy paper or cardboard. Transfer the shape of each piece to the grid, and then trace it on the wood.

Step 4. Carefully cut all parts according to the materials list. Cut all parts to exact size and cut the edges exactly square (90°). Recheck all dimensions.

Step 5. Lightly sand all surfaces and edges with medium sandpaper to remove any burrs or tool marks. Keep all edges square and sharp.

Step 6. Follow the detailed illustrations and dimensions for making the parts. Check all dimensions for accuracy; make sure both sides are exactly the same size and shape. Lay out and cut the finger joints in the top and bottom of the side, top, and bottom boards (parts 1, 2, and 3). Cut the ¾-inch-wide and ⅜-inch-deep dadoes in the sides. Take extra care to cut or route the dadoes at 90°; if they are inaccurate, it will be difficult to assemble the project. Resand with fine-grit paper, keeping all edges sharp.

Step 7. Turn the door pull (part 25) on a lathe or hand carve it as shown.

Step 8. After all the pieces have been made, dry-fit them; that is, assemble the complete project without glue or nails to check for accuracy and joint fit. If any parts fit poorly, now is the time to make corrections.

Step 9. Assemble the open hutch, keeping everything square.

Step 10. Finish to suit, using the general finishing instructions.

Pattern begins on next page.

PART	INCHES	NEEDED
1 SIDE	$3/4 \times 20^3/4 \times 68^5/8$	2
2 TOP BOARD	$3/4 \times 9^1/2 \times 32$	1
3 BOTTOM BOARD	$3/4 \times 20^3/4 \times 32$	1
4 BACK	$3/4 \times 32 \times 68^5/8$	1
5 TOP SHELF	$3/4 \times 10^1/8 \times 31^1/4$	2
6 BOTTOM SHELF	$3/4 \times 20^3/4 \times 30^1/2$	1
7 CENTER SHELF	$3/4 \times 22 \times 32$	1
8 SHELF END	$3/4 \times 1^3/4 \times 22$	2
9 DOWEL	$1/4$ DIA. $\times 3^1/4$	10
10 TOP PLATE	$3/4 \times 3 \times 32$	1
11 SIDE RAIL	$3/4 \times 5 \times 29^3/8$	2
12 TOP STILE	$3/4 \times 1^1/2 \times 22$	1
13 DOOR STOP	$3/4 \times 2 \times 30^1/2$	1
14 FRONT LEG	$3/4 \times 6 \times 33^{17}/32$	1
15 SIDE LEG	$3/4 \times 6 \times 25$	2
16 BACK LEG	$3/4 \times 5^5/8 \times 32$	1
17 TOP, FRONT	$3/4 \times 5 \times 36$	1
18 TOP, SIDE	$3/4 \times 5 \times 11^1/2$	2
19 FRONT MOLDING	$3/4 \times 7/8 \times 33^{25}/32$	1
20 SIDE MOLDING	$3/4 \times 7/8 \times 10^3/8$	2
21 DOOR RAIL	$3/4 \times 3^1/2 \times 27^1/2$	2
22 DOOR STILE	$3/4 \times 3^1/2 \times 17^1/2$	2
23 DOOR PANEL	$1/2 \times 16 \times 21^1/2$	1
24 DOOR PIN	$1/4$ DIA. $\times 3/4$	8
25 DOOR PULL	$1^1/4$ DIA. $\times 3^3/8$	1
26 DOOR PIN	6d FINISH NAIL	1
27 DOOR LATCH	$5/8 \times 5/8 \times 2^5/8$	1
28 ROUND-HEAD SCREW	NO. 8—$1^1/4$	1
29 SQUARE-CUT FINISH NAIL	2	AS REQ'D
30 HINGE (BRASS)	$2^1/2$	2

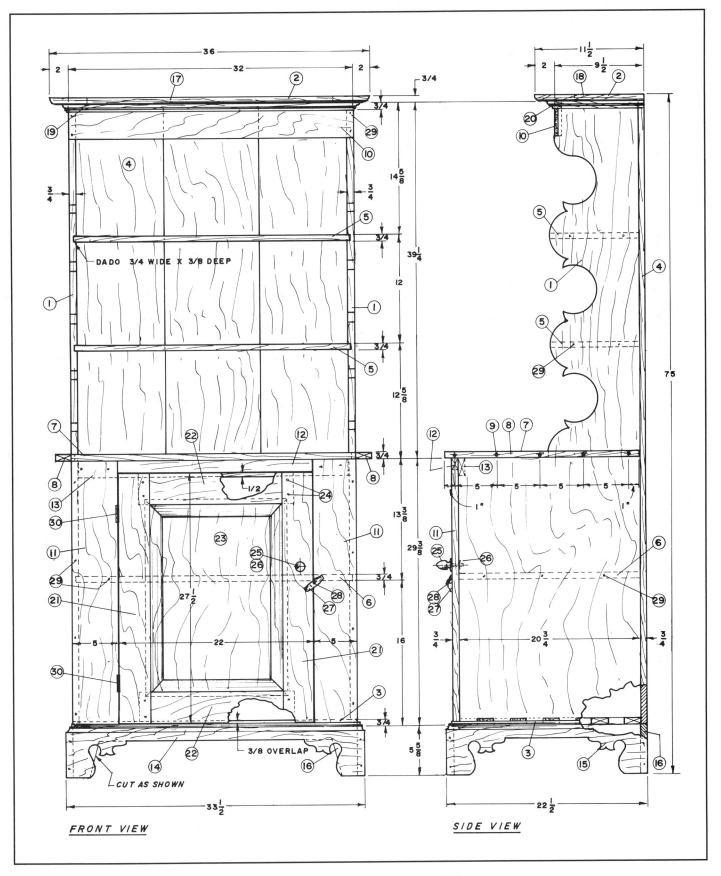

DADO 3/4 WIDE X 3/8 DEEP

CUT AS SHOWN

3/8 OVERLAP

FRONT VIEW

SIDE VIEW

143

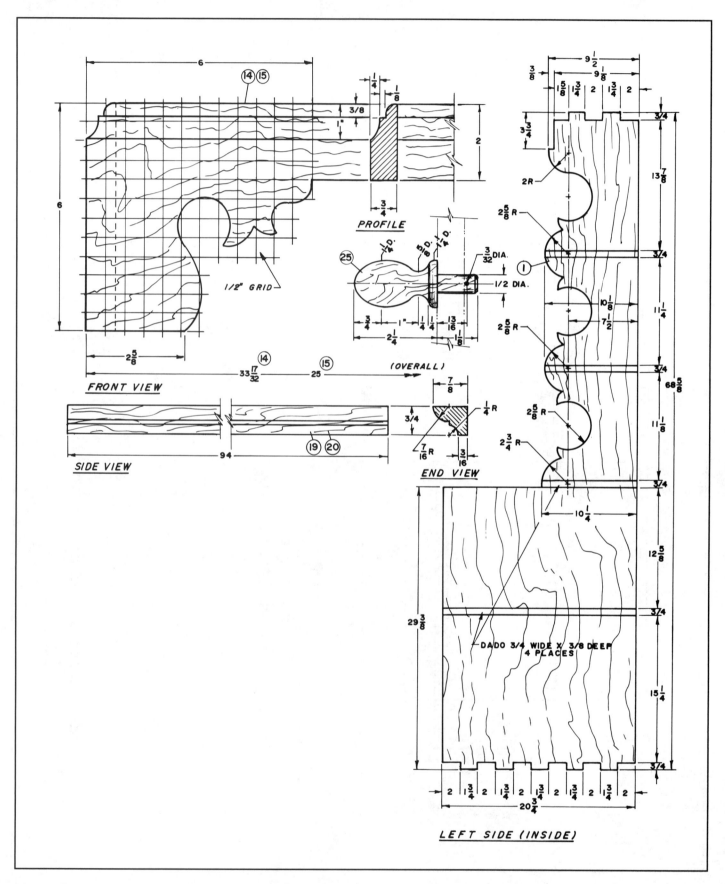

6

14 15

3/8

1"

1/4

1/8

2

3/4

PROFILE

6

1/2" GRID

2 5/8

14   15

33 17/32   25

(OVERALL)

FRONT VIEW

25

1/2 D.

3/8 D.

1 1/2 D.

3/32 DIA.

1/2 DIA.

3/4

1"

1/4

1/4

13/16

1/8

2 1/4

94

19 20

3/4

7/8

1/4 R

7/16 R

3/16

SIDE VIEW

END VIEW

9 1/2

9 1/8

3/8

1 5/8   1 3/4   2   1 3/4   2

3/4

3 3/4

2R

2 5/8 R

1

2 5/8 R

2 5/8 R

2 3/4 R

13 7/8

3/4

10 1/8

7 1/2

11 1/4

3/4

68 3/8

11 1/8

3/4

10 1/4

12 5/8

3/4

DADO 3/4 WIDE X 3/8 DEEP
4 PLACES

29 3/8

15 1/4

3/4

2   1 3/4   2   1 3/4   2   1 3/4   2   1 3/4   2   1 3/4   2

20 3/4

LEFT SIDE (INSIDE)

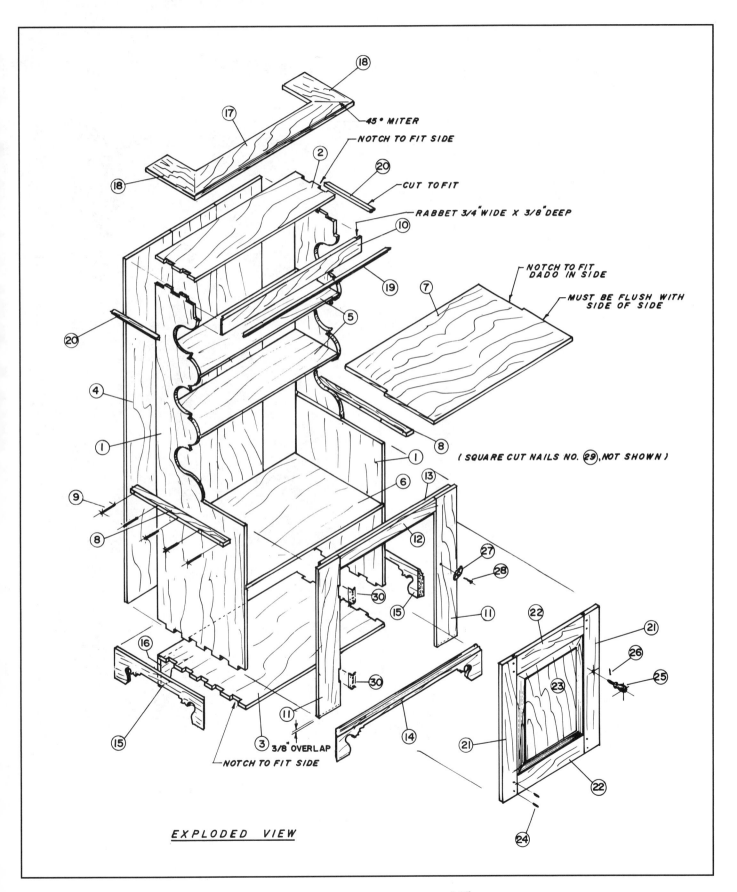

45° MITER

NOTCH TO FIT SIDE

CUT TO FIT

RABBET 3/4" WIDE X 3/8" DEEP

NOTCH TO FIT
DADO IN SIDE

MUST BE FLUSH WITH
SIDE OF SIDE

(SQUARE CUT NAILS NO. 29, NOT SHOWN)

3/8" OVERLAP

NOTCH TO FIT SIDE

EXPLODED VIEW

Chimney Cupboard

Early New England homes were not always well designed; for example, it was not uncommon to find a chimney running through the middle of a second-floor bedroom. Chimney chests, like this one, were built thin and tall so that they could be placed against the chimney to divide the room—and look better than the chimney alone. Today this cupboard is perfect for storage; it takes up little floor space and has more than 10 feet of shelf space. The original, made of maple with a light stain, was found in Hillsborough Center, New Hampshire. Most chimney cupboards, however, were made of pine, and many were painted.

Step 1. Study the plans carefully, checking the shape of each part. Visualize how you will make the chimney cupboard and what tools you will need.

Step 2. As you study the plans, note the order in which the project is to be assembled.

Step 3. Carefully cut all parts according to the materials list. It is extremely important to cut all parts to exact size and cut the edges exactly square (90°). When cutting multiple parts, such as the shelves (part 2), use saw stops if possible so that all parts are exactly the same length. The sides (part 1) are the most important part of the cupboard, so take extra care in making these. Cut the eight dadoes ¾ inch wide and ¼ inch deep as shown. Cut a rabbet ½ inch wide and ¼ inch deep along the entire back edge of both pieces. Be sure to make a matching pair of sides, one right and one left. Recheck all dimensions.

Step 4. Glue together material for the back (part 3). Glue and nail the sides (part 1), the shelves (part 2), and the back. For that very old look, use square-cut nails and do not countersink them. Remember, in antique furniture the nails were often left showing. If you want a more "finished" look, use 8d finish nails and countersink and fill them. Check that the case is absolutely square.

Step 5. Add the remaining case pieces. The molding does not have to be exactly as shown; if you don't have a router or shaper, you can purchase commercial molding similar to that shown. If you have a shaper, you might want to make the top molding one piece instead of the three pieces shown (parts 12, 13, and 14).

Step 6. The doors are made to fit the top and bottom openings. Your openings might vary slightly, so check the dimensions carefully. Cut a groove along the inside edge of the door ¼-inch wide and ½-inch deep. Cut a groove ½-inch wide and 1-inch deep about 3 inches in from each end of parts 15 and 18. On the ends of the nails (parts 16 and 19), cut a tongue ¼-inch wide and 1-inch long. Cut the panels (parts 17 and 20) to size and sand all over.

Step 7. After all the pieces have been made, dry-fit them; that is, assemble the complete project without glue or nails to check for accuracy and joint fit. If any parts fit poorly, now is the time to make corrections. Glue and nail the parts together except the panels, which should "float" to allow for expansion. Add the doors, using the hinges (part 21). Notch the right side (part 4) for the hinges as shown.

Step 8. The pull (part 22) can be turned on a lathe or carved out. It doesn't have to be exact, just close to the one shown. The stop or latch (part 23) is pinned in place with a finish nail, as shown in the door pull detail. It should be placed so that it turns freely and holds the bottom door closed. Take care that it does not get too close to the shelf.

Step 9. Mortise or carve out the top door lock (part 25).

Step 10. Finish to suit, using the general finishing instructions.

Pattern begins on next page.

PART	INCHES	NEEDED
1 SIDE	$3/4 \times 10^{1}/_{4} \times 89^{1}/_{4}$	2
2 SHELF	$3/4 \times 10^{1}/_{4} \times 17^{1}/_{2}$	8
3 BACK	$1/2 \times 17^{1}/_{2} \times 89^{1}/_{4}$	1
4 FRONT STILE	$3/4 \times 3^{1}/_{4} \times 89^{1}/_{4}$	2
5 FRONT RAIL	$3/4 \times 2^{1}/_{4} \times 12$	2
6 FRONT SPACER	$3/4 \times 2^{3}/_{4} \times 12$	1
7 DOOR STOP	$1/2 \times 2^{3}/_{4} \times 17$	1
8 DOOR STOP	$1/2 \times 2^{1}/_{2} \times 17$	1
9 DIVIDER	$3/4 \times 1 \times 48$	1
10 TOP BOARD	$3/4 \times 4^{1}/_{2} \times 54$	1
11 MOLDING	$3/4 \times 3/4 \times 48$	1
12 MOLDING	$3/4 \times 1^{3}/_{4} \times 50$	1
13 MOLDING	$1/2 \times 1 \times 50$	1
14 MOLDING $1/4$ ROUND	$1/2 \times 1/2 \times 50$	1
15 DOOR STILE	$3/4 \times 2^{1}/_{4} \times 55$	2
16 DOOR RAIL	$3/4 \times 2^{1}/_{2} \times 9^{1}/_{2}$	4
17 TOP PANEL	$1/4 \times 8^{3}/_{8} \times 15^{7}/_{8}$	3
18 DOOR STILE	$3/4 \times 2^{1}/_{4} \times 21$	2
19 DOOR RAIL	$3/4 \times 3 \times 9^{1}/_{2}$	2
20 BOTTOM PANEL	$1/4 \times 8^{3}/_{8} \times 15^{7}/_{8}$	1
21 HINGE (BRASS)	3	4
22 PULL	1 DIA. $\times 3^{1}/_{2}$	1
23 STOP	$3/8 \times 1 \times 2^{1}/_{2}$	1
24 PIN	LENGTH TO SUIT	1
25 DOOR LOCK	LENGTH TO SUIT	1

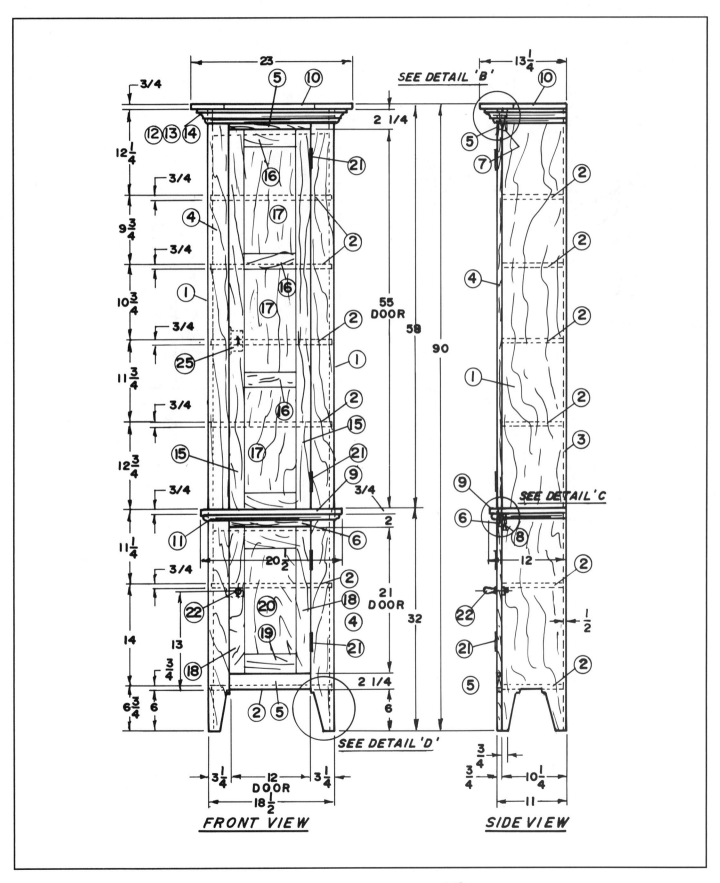

FRONT VIEW

SIDE VIEW

149

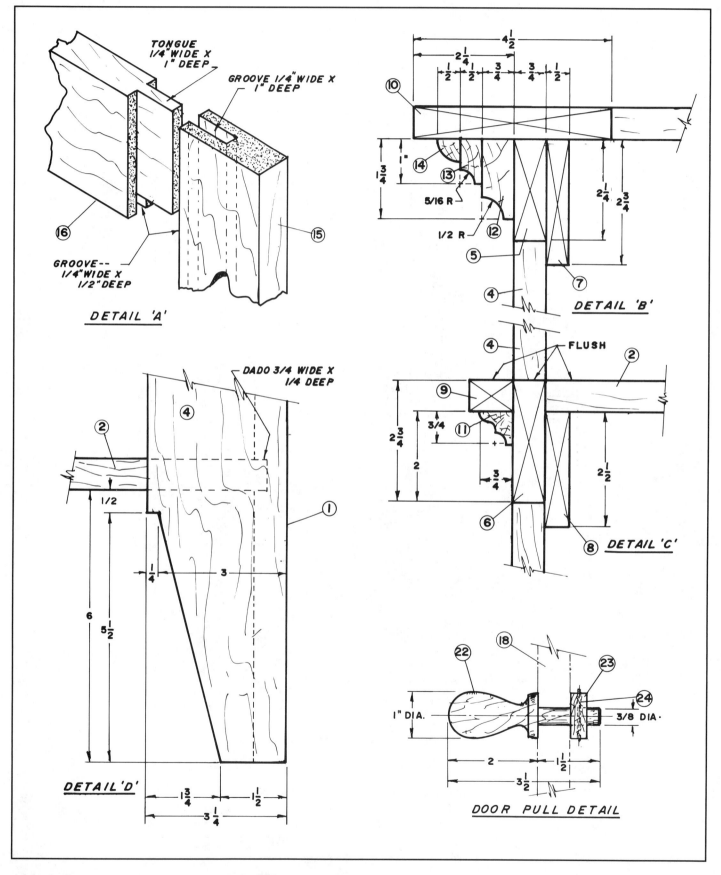

TONGUE
1/4" WIDE X
1" DEEP

GROOVE 1/4" WIDE X
1" DEEP

GROOVE --
1/4" WIDE X
1/2" DEEP

DETAIL 'A'

16   15

4 1/2
2 1/4
1/2   1/2   3/4   3/4   1/2

10
14
13
5/16 R
1/2 R
12
5
4
7
1 3/4
1"
2 1/4
2 3/4

DETAIL 'B'

DADO 3/4 WIDE X
1/4 DEEP

2   4

1/2

1/4   3

6   5 1/2

DETAIL 'D'

1 3/4   1/2
3 1/4

1

4   FLUSH   2
9
11
2 3/4   3/4   2
3/4
2 1/2
6
8   DETAIL 'C'

22   18   23   24
1" DIA.
3/8 DIA.
2   1 1/2
3 1/2

DOOR PULL DETAIL

150

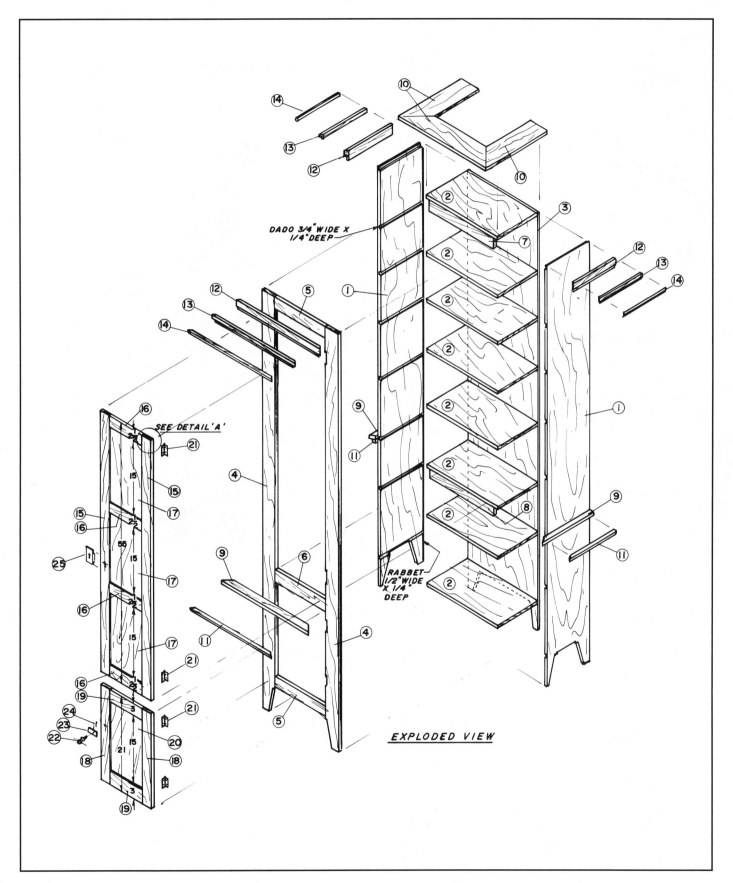

DADO 3/4" WIDE X 1/4" DEEP

SEE DETAIL 'A'

RABBET 1/2" WIDE X 1/4" DEEP

EXPLODED VIEW

Pennsylvania Pillar and Scroll Shelf Clock

This is a smaller version of a clock made by Jacob D. Custer of Norristown, Pennsylvania. The original was constructed in 1832 of mahogany veneer. It had a brass, eight-day, weight-driven time and strike moon phase and calendar movement, which was a very sophisticated movement for its time. Although the original was 17 inches wide and 34½ inches high, I scaled my copy (made of walnut) down to 13½ inches wide and 28 inches high for today's smaller homes.

Since the original has a beautiful painted dial, my wife, Joyce, copied it as closely as possible. Our moon section is false and painted on, and because we used a quartz movement, the key-wind holes are false. Years ago many tall case clocks had false keyholes to give an inexpensive pull-wind clock an expensive key-wind look. If you don't want to paint the dial face, get your dial custom painted.

Because I repair and collect unique clocks, I enjoyed this project. This is a very rare pillar and scroll clock, a model I have always wanted but couldn't afford, even if I could find one for sale. This clock takes its place among the hundreds of copies of beautiful Eli Terry pillar and scroll clocks, some of which were crafted by Seth Thomas.

If you don't have a lathe, purchase custom-made turnings (parts 15, 23, 24, and 34) from Riverbend Turnings (see the list of suppliers). The company will make them from any wood for a reasonable price.

Step 1. Study the plans carefully, checking the shape of each part. Visualize how you will make the clock and what tools you will need.

Step 2. As you study the plans, note the order in which the project is to be assembled. The case is not much more than a box with moldings and turnings added to it.

Step 3. The parts that have irregular shapes should be laid out on a ½-inch grid to make a full-size pattern on heavy paper or cardboard. Transfer the shape of each piece to the grid, and then trace it on the wood.

Step 4. Carefully cut all parts according to the materials list. Cut all parts to exact size and cut the edges exactly square (90°). Recheck all dimensions.

Step 5. Lightly sand all surfaces and edges with medium sandpaper to remove any burrs or tool marks. Keep all edges square and sharp.

Step 6. Follow the detailed illustrations and dimensions for making the parts. Check all dimensions for accuracy. Resand with fine-grit paper, keeping all edges sharp.

Step 7. Make the moldings now. To make the goose neck molding (part 20), use the goose neck (part 16) as a pattern so that it will fit exactly. Make more molding than you need in case you make an error in the miter cuts.

Step 8. After all the pieces have been made, dry-fit them; that is, assemble the complete project without glue or nails to check for accuracy and joint fit. If any parts fit poorly, now is the time to make corrections.

Step 9. Glue together; double-check that the case is exactly square before the glue sets. Make the pieces for the door to fit the case opening. If you made any errors in the layout of the case, fit the door to it.

Step 10. Lay out the dial and paint it according to the illustration. Remember it does not have to be perfect or exactly as illustrated—use your imagination.

Step 11. Assemble the clock, keeping everything square. Temporarily add all hardware and the movement, including the hands. Check that the door fits and opens correctly.

Step 12. Remove all hardware and finish to suit, using the general finishing instructions.

Step 13. Cut glass to fit the two sides and door; set as you would any glass. For an old look, use a gray or black glazing compound.

Step 14. Reattach the hardware. Attach the quartz movement to the dial face and attach the face to the inside of the case. Use simple filler blocks made from scrap wood to support the dial face and movement. The hands should be positioned just inside the glass.

Pattern begins on next page.

PART		INCHES	NEEDED
1	SIDE	$1/2 \times 3^{11}/_{16} \times 18$	2
2	BOTTOM	$1/2 \times 3^{7}/_{16} \times 10^{5}/_{8}$	1
3	TOP	$1/2 \times 3^{11}/_{16} \times 12^{3}/_{8}$	1
4	EAR	$3/4 \times 3^{11}/_{16} \times 3$	2
5	BACK	$1/4 \times 10^{5}/_{8} \times 18$	1
6	FLAT-HEAD SCREW	NO. 8—$3/4$—BRASS	6
7	BRACKET	$1/2 \times 3^{7}/_{16} \times 4^{15}/_{16}$	2
8	SPACER	$1/2 \times 3^{1}/_{2} \times 12^{3}/_{8}$	1
9	BOTTOM FRONT	$3/4 \times 1^{3}/_{8} \times 13^{5}/_{8}$	1
10	BOTTOM SIDE	$3/4 \times 1^{3}/_{8} \times 4^{13}/_{16}$	2
11	BLOCK	$3/4 \times 1^{1}/_{4} \times 1^{1}/_{8}$	4
12	FRONT BASE	$1/8 \times 1^{3}/_{8} \times 13^{7}/_{8}$	1
13	SIDE BASE	$1/8 \times 1^{3}/_{8} \times 4^{7}/_{8}$	2
14	FILLER BASE	$1/4 \times 4^{3}/_{16} \times 12^{1}/_{2}$	1
15	FOOT	$1^{1}/_{8}$ DIA. $\times 3$	4
16	GOOSE NECK	$5/8 \times 6^{13}/_{16} \times 10^{1}/_{8}$	2
17	SIDE TOP	$5/8 \times 3^{1}/_{2} \times 4^{5}/_{8}$	2
18	CENTER TRIM	$1/4 \times 1 \times 2^{1}/_{4}$	1
19	TOP TRIM	$1/8 \times 1 \times 1^{1}/_{4}$	1
20	FRONT MOLDING	$3/8 \times 3^{1}/_{2} \times 9$	2
21	SIDE MOLDING	$3/8 \times 1/2 \times 5^{1}/_{4}$	2
22	PIN	$1/8$ DIA. $\times 1^{1}/_{8}$	2
23	ROSETTE	$1^{3}/_{8}$ DIA. $\times 3/8$	2
24	FINIAL	$7/8$ DIA. $\times 3$	3
25	STILE	$1/2 \times 1^{1}/_{4} \times 14^{3}/_{4}$	2
26	BOTTOM RAIL	$1/2 \times 1 \times 9^{7}/_{8}$	1
27	CENTER RAIL	$1/2 \times 7/8 \times 9^{7}/_{8}$	1
28	TOP RAIL	$1/2 \times 4^{1}/_{2} \times 9^{7}/_{8}$	1
29	HINGE	NO. 2506-B	2
30	FLAT-HEAD SCREW	LENGTH TO SUIT	4
31	PANEL	$1/4 \times 3^{7}/_{8} \times 8^{13}/_{16}$	1
32	GLASS	$3/32 \times 2^{7}/_{16}$ DIA.	1
33	GLASS	$3/32 \times 8^{13}/_{16} \times 12^{1}/_{4}$	1
34	COLUMN	$7/8 \times 7/8 \times 15^{1}/_{2}$	4
35	PIN-HINGE (BRASS)	$5/8$	2
36	SIDE GLASS	$3/32 \times 2^{3}/_{16} \times 6^{9}/_{16}$	2
37	DIAL SUPPORT	$3/4 \times 3/4 \times 3$	4
38	DIAL	$1/4 \times 9^{1}/_{2} \times 12^{15}/_{16}$	1
39	MOVEMENT (7 LG.)	NO. 3722-X	1
40	HANDS (4 LG.)	NO. 4938-X	1 PAIR
41	MAGNETIC CATCH	NO. 2552-X	1
42	PULL $1/2$ DIA. (BRASS)	NO. 2525-B	1

NOTE: IF POSSIBLE, HANDS (PART 40) SHOULD BE MADE FROM STEEL, NOT PURCHASED.

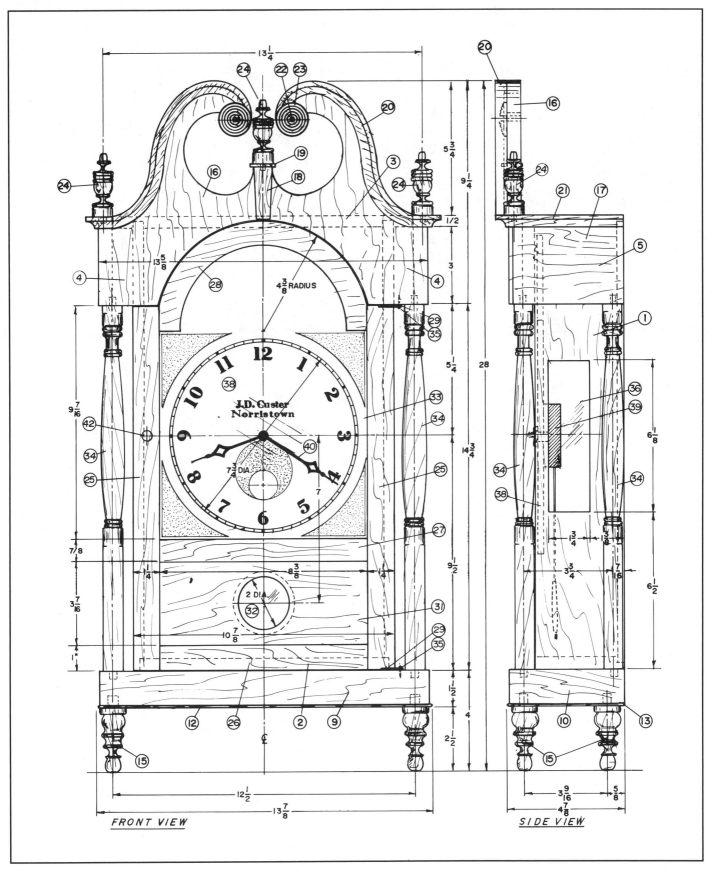

FRONT VIEW

SIDE VIEW

155

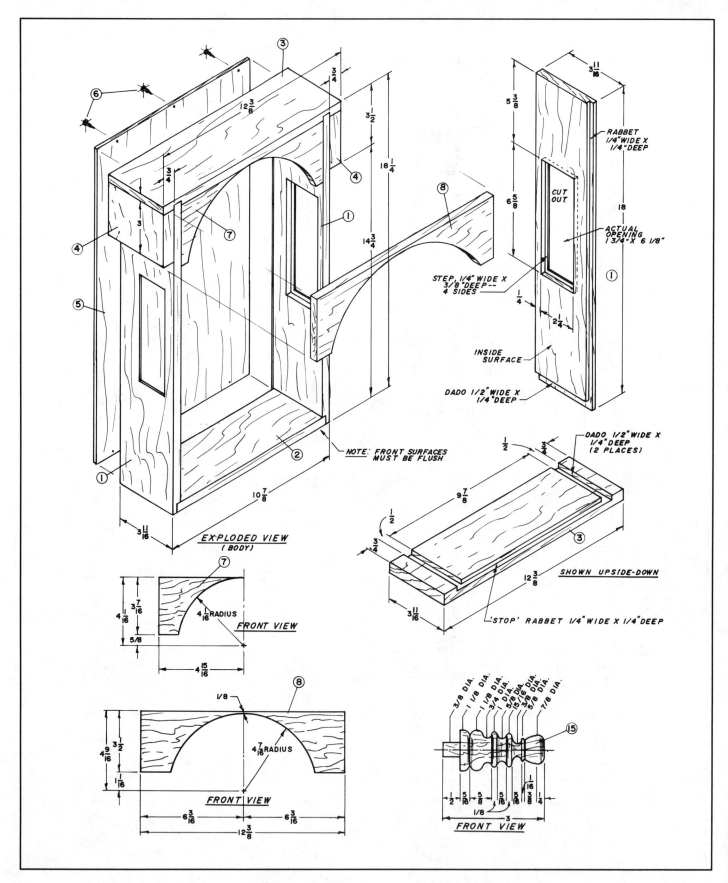

EXPLODED VIEW
(BODY)

NOTE: FRONT SURFACES
MUST BE FLUSH

RABBET
1/4" WIDE X
1/4" DEEP

CUT
OUT

ACTUAL
OPENING
1 3/4" X 6 1/8"

INSIDE
SURFACE

DADO 1/2" WIDE X
1/4" DEEP

STEP, 1/4" WIDE X
3/8" DEEP --
4 SIDES

DADO 1/2" WIDE X
1/4" DEEP
(2 PLACES)

SHOWN UPSIDE-DOWN

'STOP' RABBET 1/4" WIDE X 1/4" DEEP

FRONT VIEW

4 1/4" RADIUS

FRONT VIEW

4 7/16 RADIUS

FRONT VIEW

156

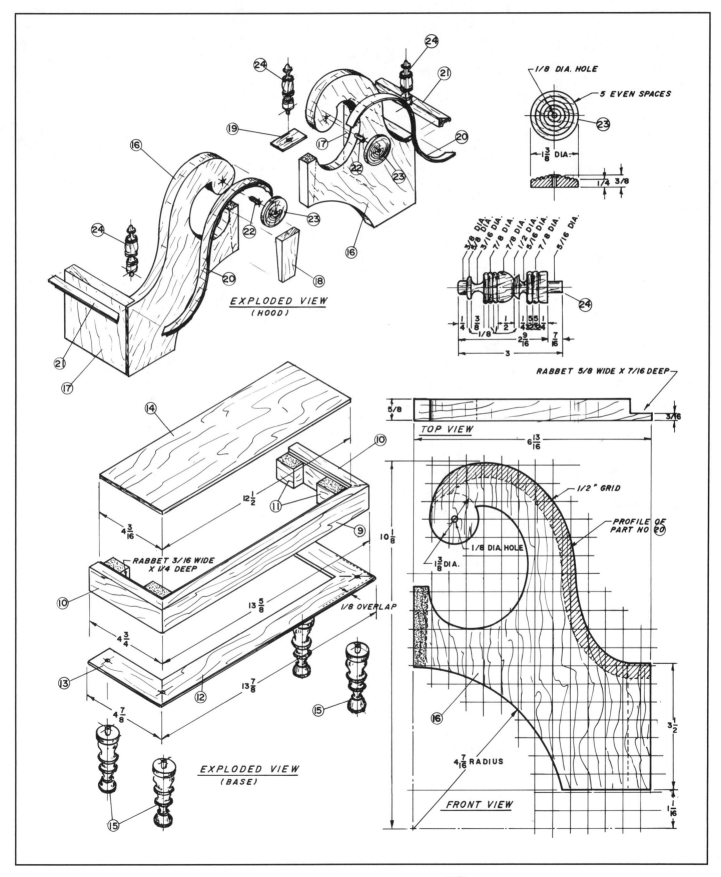

1/8 DIA. HOLE

5 EVEN SPACES

23

1 3/8 DIA.

1/4 3/8

3/8 DIA.
3/8 DIA.
3/16 DIA.
7/8 DIA.
7/8 DIA.
1/2 DIA.
5/16 DIA.
7/8 DIA.
5/16 DIA.

24

1/4
3/8
1/8
1/2
5
1 2 3 4
5/16
7/16

2 9/16

3

EXPLODED VIEW
(HOOD)

RABBET 5/8 WIDE X 7/16 DEEP

5/8

TOP VIEW

3/16

6 13/16

1/2" GRID

PROFILE OF
PART NO 20

1/8 DIA. HOLE

1 3/8 DIA.

12 1/2

RABBET 3/16 WIDE
X 1/4 DEEP

4 3/16

13 5/8

1/8 OVERLAP

10 1/8

4 3/4

13 7/8

4 7/8

EXPLODED VIEW
(BASE)

4 7/16 RADIUS

3 1/2

1 1/16

FRONT VIEW

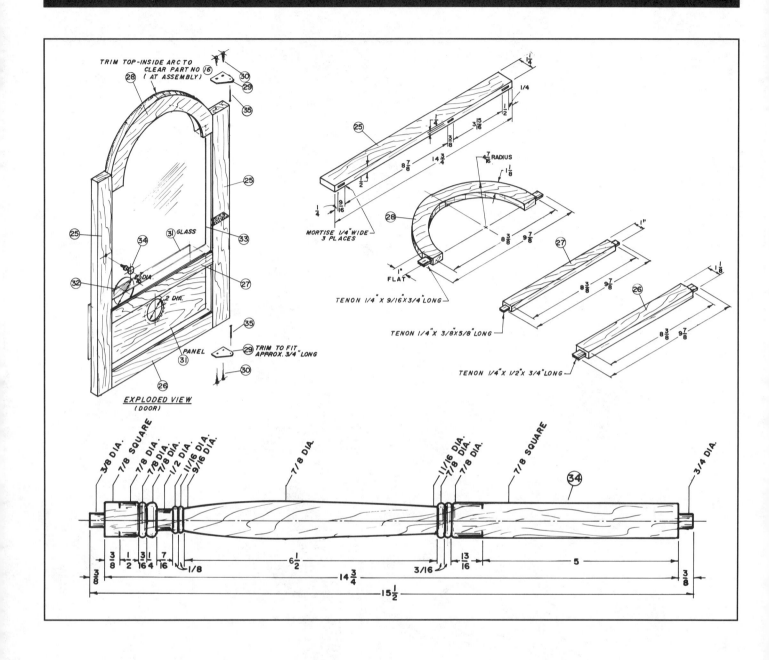

TRIM TOP-INSIDE ARC TO
CLEAR PART NO (16)
(AT ASSEMBLY)

GLASS

½ DIA.

2 DIA.

PANEL

TRIM TO FIT
APPROX. 3/4" LONG

EXPLODED VIEW
(DOOR)

MORTISE 1/4" WIDE
3 PLACES

TENON 1/4" X 9/16"X3/4"LONG

FLAT

4 7/16 RADIUS

1⅛

8⅜ 9⅞

TENON 1/4" X 3/8X5/8" LONG

1"

8⅜ 9⅞

1⅛

8⅜ 9⅞

TENON 1/4"X 1/2"X 3/4"LONG

14¾

8⅞

3/8 DIA.
7/8 SQUARE
7/8 DIA.
7/8 DIA.
7/8 DIA.
1/2 DIA.
11/16 DIA.
9/16 DIA.

7/8 DIA.

11/16 DIA.
7/8 DIA.
7/8 DIA.

7/8 SQUARE

3/4 DIA.

3/8 1/2 3/16¼ 7/16

1/8

6½

3/16

13/16

5

3/8

3/8

14¾

15½

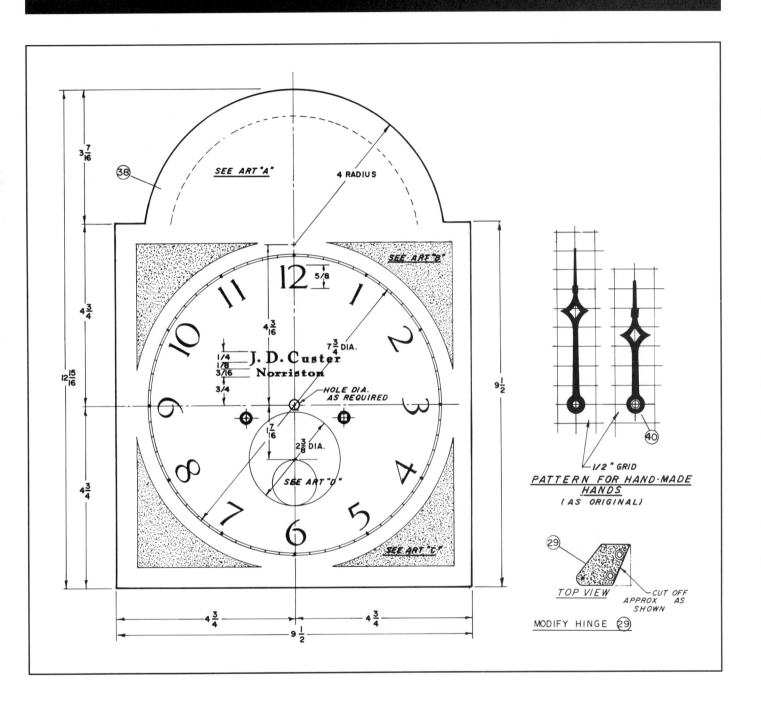

3 7/16
38
SEE ART "A"
4 RADIUS

4 3/4
SEE ART "B"

12 15/16
12
5/8
4 3/16
7 3/4 DIA.
1/4
1/8
3/16
J. D. Custer
Norriston
3/4
HOLE DIA.
AS REQUIRED
7/16
2 3/8 DIA.
SEE ART "D"

9 1/2

4 3/4
SEE ART "C"

4 3/4   4 3/4
9 1/2

1/2" GRID
40
PATTERN FOR HAND-MADE
HANDS
(AS ORIGINAL)

29
TOP VIEW
CUT OFF
APPROX AS
SHOWN
MODIFY HINGE 29

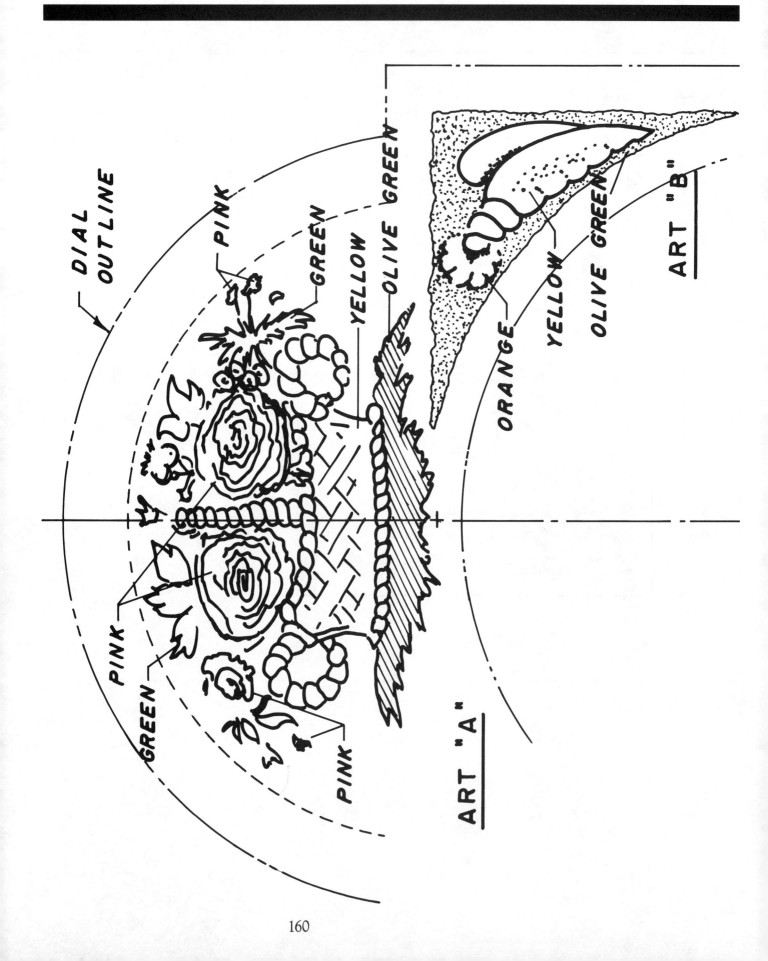

DIAL OUTLINE

PINK

PINK

GREEN

YELLOW

OLIVE GREEN

ORANGE

YELLOW

OLIVE GREEN

ART "B"

PINK

GREEN

PINK

ART "A"

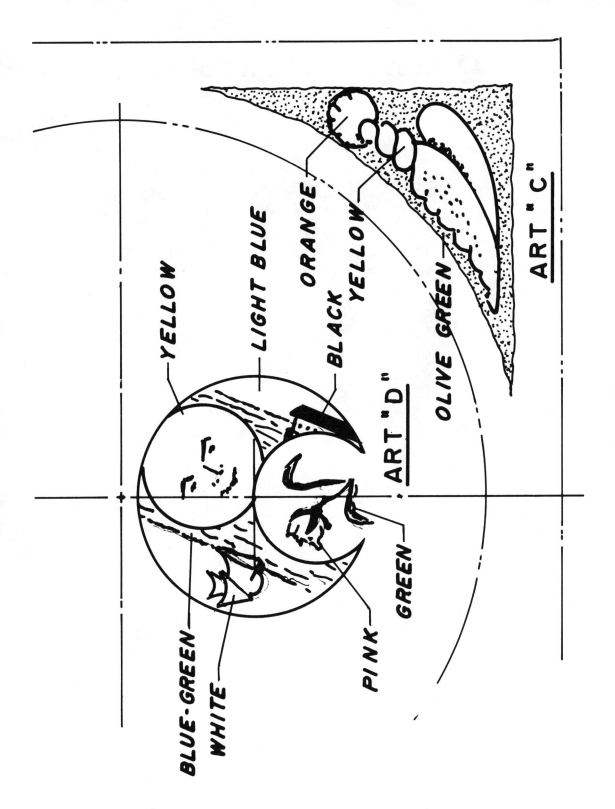

YELLOW

LIGHT BLUE

ORANGE

BLACK

YELLOW

OLIVE GREEN

ART "C"

ART "D"

BLUE-GREEN

WHITE

PINK

GREEN

Queen Anne Lowboy

During the Queen Anne period, from 1725 to 1760, cabinetmakers combined Chinese and Japanese elements with the cyma curve from the William and Mary period (1690 to 1725), the cabriole leg, the shell carving, and the ball-and-claw foot. Queen Anne style was lighter and much more graceful than previous furniture designs. Drawers incorporated an overhanging lip—a new idea for drawer design—and the new rule joint for drop-leaf tables was developed.

Craftsmen of various areas preferred different types of wood for making their cabinets. For example, in most of New England maple was used; in Pennsylvania, walnut; and in North and South Carolina, cypress. The use of regional woods continued throughout the Queen Anne era, which was followed by the Chippendale era (1760 to 1780).

The cabriole legs are very easy to make if you have a band saw. They are simply laid out and cut, and a wood rasp is used to round all the edges. A detailed, dimensioned drawing is provided for laying out the legs, but a much simpler way to obtain them is to purchase them. Beautiful sets of completely finished legs (part number AFR-34) can be bought from Adams Wood Products, Inc. (see the list of suppliers) in cherry, red oak, mahogany, or walnut.

Step 1. Study the plans carefully, checking the shape of each part. Visualize how you will make the Queen Anne lowboy and what tools you will need. If you plan to make the legs (part 1), study the double saw-cut method of band sewing in a technical woodworking book.

Step 2. As you study the plans, note the order in which the project is to be assembled.

Step 3. Since the legs and the front panel (parts 1 and 4) have irregular shapes, they should be laid out on a 1-inch grid to make a full-size pattern on heavy paper or cardboard. Transfer the shape of each piece to the grid, and then trace it on the wood.

Step 4. Carefully cut all parts according to the materials list. Cut all parts to exact size and cut the edges exactly square (90°). Recheck all dimensions.

Step 5. Lightly sand all surfaces and edges with medium sandpaper to remove any burrs or tool marks. Keep all edges square and sharp.

Step 6. Follow the detailed illustrations and dimensions for making the parts. Check all dimensions for accuracy. Resand with fine-grit paper, keeping all edges sharp. When you cut the drawer parts, use saw stops so that all matching parts will be exactly the same size and shape. If you purchased the legs, cut off 10½ inches and a mortise for the front panel, back, and stretchers, (parts 4, 2, and 3); refer to the exploded view for details. Double-check all layout work for accuracy before cutting the mortises.

Step 7. After all the pieces have been made, dry-fit them; that is, assemble the complete project without glue or nails to check for accuracy and joint fit. If any parts fit poorly, now is the time to make corrections.

Step 8. Assemble the lowboy, keeping everything square. Carefully add the interior drawer supports, one at a time, and check all dimensions as you add the pieces. Make the drawers and use them as a guide in adding the drawer supports. These interior parts are screwed in place, not glued, so you can always readjust them.

Step 9. Finish to suit, using the general finishing instructions.

Pattern begins on next page.

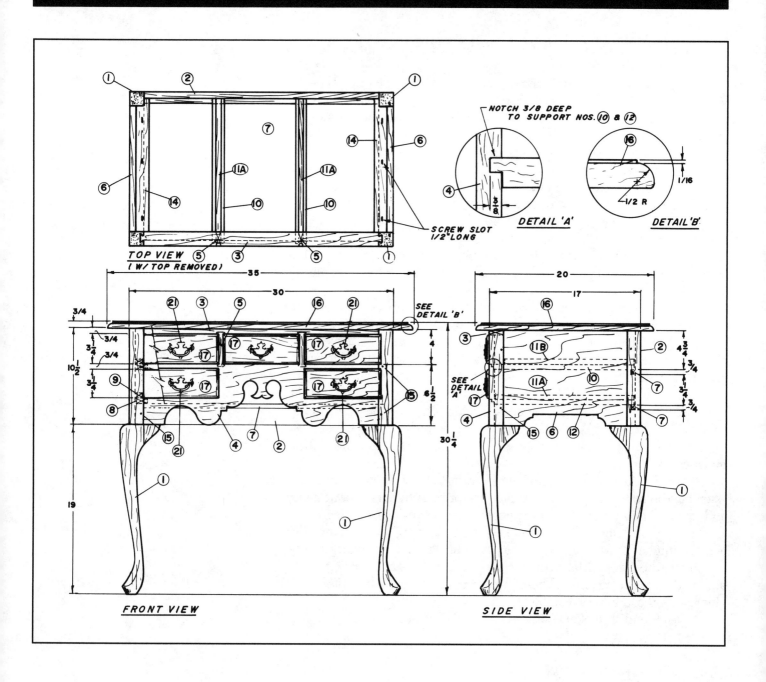

NOTCH 3/8 DEEP
TO SUPPORT NOS. ⑩ & ⑫

SCREW SLOT
1/2" LONG

DETAIL 'A'

DETAIL 'B'

1/16

1/2 R

TOP VIEW
(W/ TOP REMOVED)

SEE DETAIL 'B'

FRONT VIEW

SEE DETAIL 'A'

SIDE VIEW

164

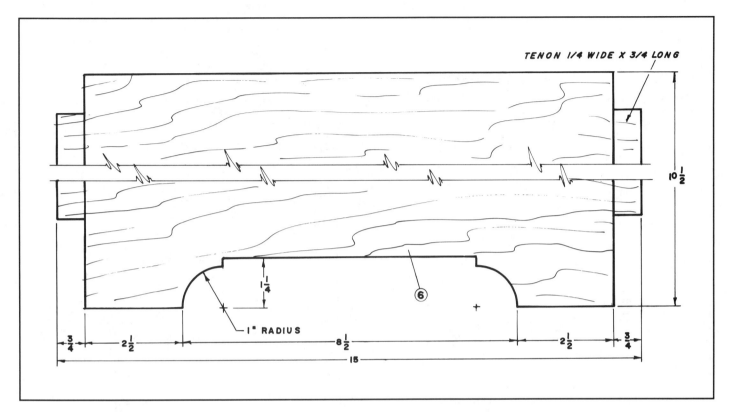

TENON 1/4 WIDE X 3/4 LONG

10½

1¼

1" RADIUS

⑥

¾ 2½ 8½ 2½ ¾

15

PART	INCHES	NEEDED
*1 LEG	$2^3/_4 \times 2^3/_4 \times 29^1/_2$	4
2 BACK	$3/_4 \times 10^1/_2 \times 28$	1
*3 STRETCHER	$3/_4 \times 1^3/_4 \times 27^1/_2$	1
*4 FRONT PANEL	$3/_4 \times 6^1/_2 \times 28$	1
*5 DIVIDER	$3/_4 \times 1^3/_4 \times 4$	2
*6 END PANEL	$3/_4 \times 10^1/_2 \times 15$	2
7 SUPPORT	$3/_4 \times 3/_4 \times 26^1/_2$	2
8 DRAWER SUPPORT	$3/_4 \times 1^1/_2 \times 15^1/_2$	4
9 DRAWER GUIDE	$3/_4 \times 1 \times 13^1/_2$	4
10 DRAWER SUPPORT	$3/_4 \times 1^3/_4 \times 15^7/_8$	2
11A DRAWER GUIDE	$3/_4 \times 3/_4 \times 15^1/_2$	2
11B DRAWER GUIDE	$3/_4 \times 3/_4 \times 14^5/_8$	2
12 DRAWER SUPPORT	$3/_4 \times 1^1/_4 \times 15^1/_2$	2
13 FLAT-HEAD SCREW	NO. 8—$1^3/_8$	AS REQ'D
14 TOP SUPPORT	$3/_4 \times 1^1/_2 \times 14^1/_2$	2
*15 PIN	$3/_{16}$ DIA. $\times 1^3/_4$	16
*16 TOP BOARD	$3/_4 \times 20 \times 35$	1
*17 DRAWER FRONT	$3/_4 \times 3^1/_2 \times 8^7/_8$	5
18 DRAWER SIDE	$3/_8 \times 3^1/_8 \times 14^3/_4$	10
19 DRAWER BACK	$3/_8 \times 2^5/_8 \times 7^7/_8$	5
20 DRAWER BOTTOM	$3/_8 \times 7^{13}/_{16} \times 15$	5
21 PULL	A-2702 (OR EQUAL)	5

*PRIMARY WOOD

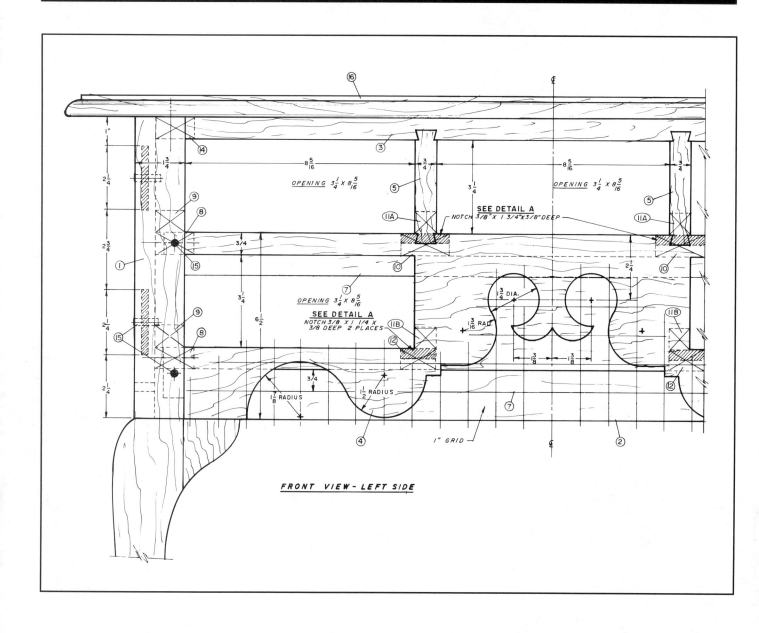

FRONT VIEW - LEFT SIDE

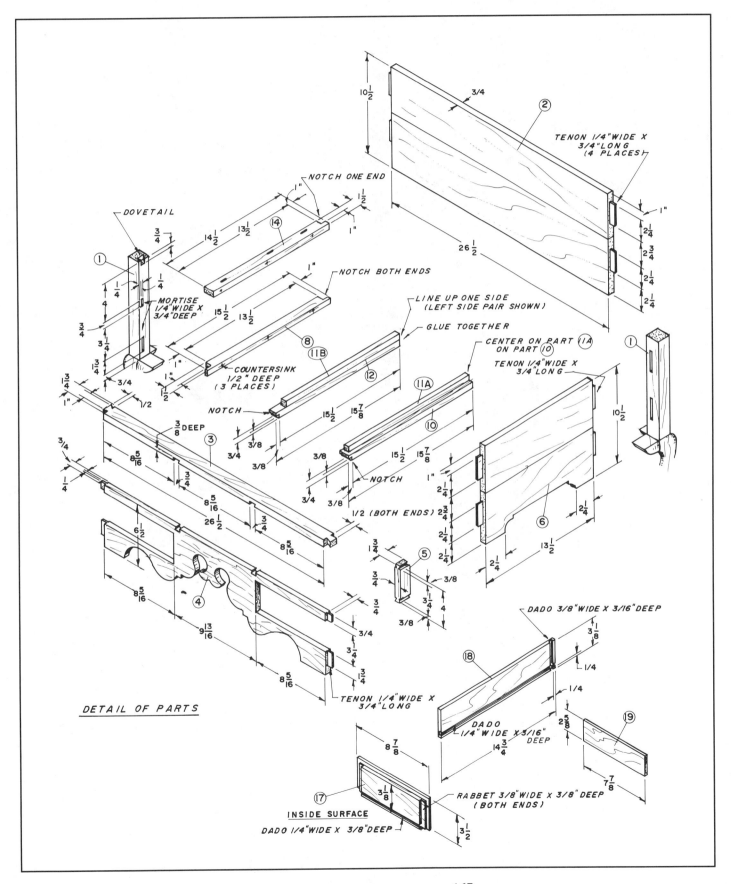

DETAIL OF PARTS

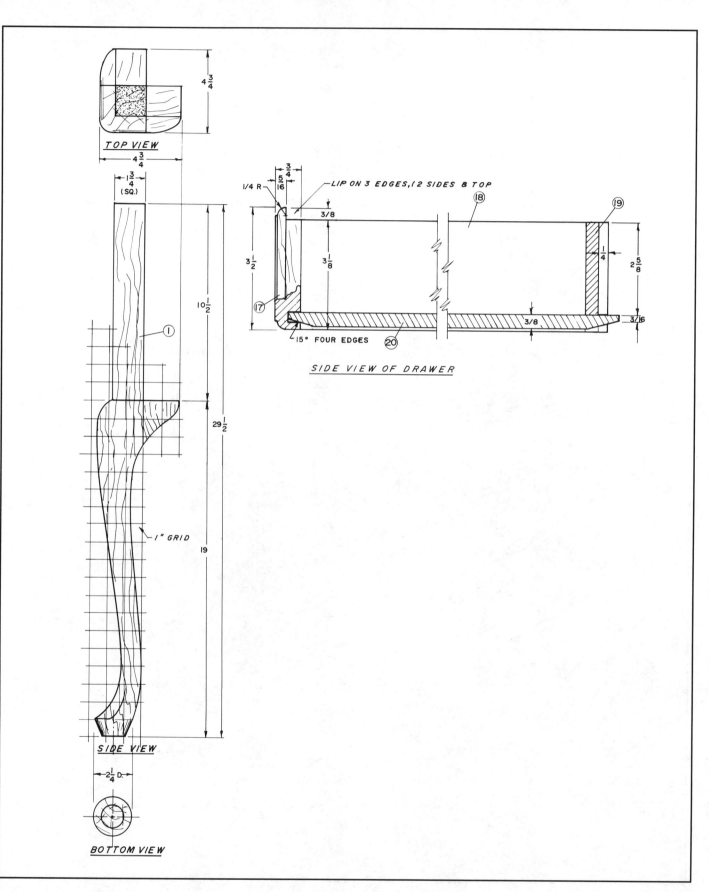

TOP VIEW

$4\frac{3}{4}$

$4\frac{3}{4}$

$1\frac{3}{4}$
(SQ.)

①

$10\frac{1}{2}$

— 1" GRID

$29\frac{1}{2}$

19

SIDE VIEW

$2\frac{1}{4}$ D.

BOTTOM VIEW

LIP ON 3 EDGES, (2 SIDES & TOP)

$\frac{3}{4}$

$\frac{5}{16}$

1/4 R

3/8

$3\frac{1}{2}$

$3\frac{1}{8}$

⑰

15° FOUR EDGES

⑳

⑱

⑲

$\frac{1}{4}$

$2\frac{5}{8}$

3/8

3/16

SIDE VIEW OF DRAWER

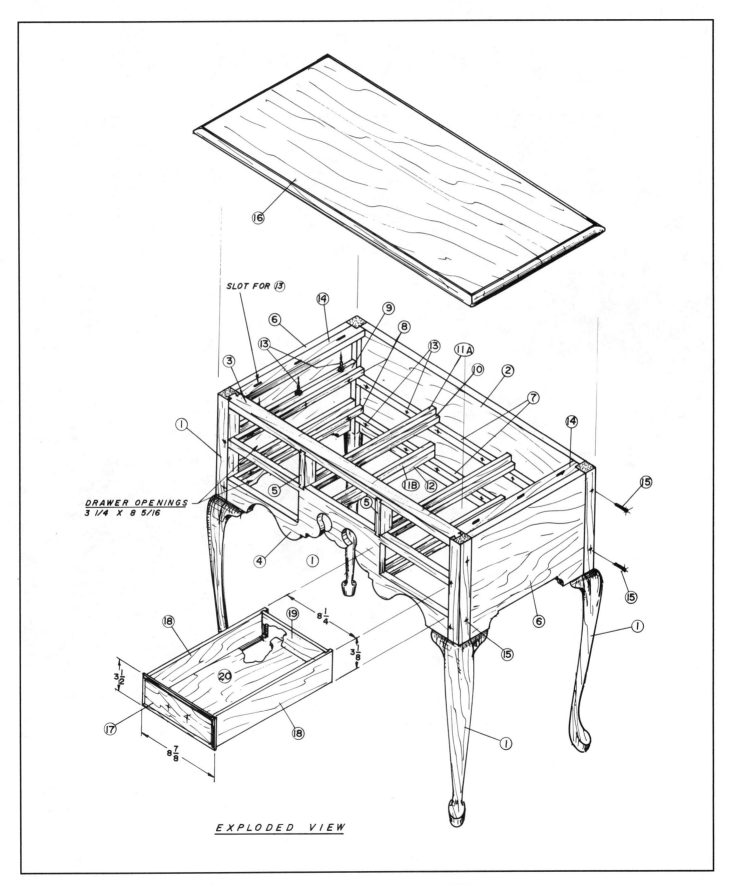

SLOT FOR ⑬

⑭

⑥

⑬

⑨

⑧

⑬

⑪A

③

⑩ ②

⑦

①

⑭

DRAWER OPENINGS
3 1/4 X 8 5/16

⑤

⑮

⑤

⑪B ⑫

④

①

⑮

⑥

⑱

⑲

$8\frac{1}{4}$

⑥

①

$3\frac{1}{8}$

⑳

⑮

$3\frac{1}{2}$

⑰

⑱

①

$8\frac{7}{8}$

EXPLODED VIEW

169

Pencil-Post Bed

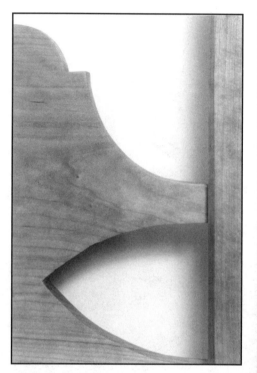

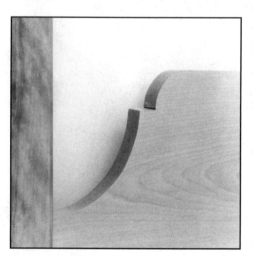

One way to change the appearance of a bed is to vary the style of its headboard. The headboard at top is shown on pages 173 and 174. At bottom is the headboard shown on page 177.

In Colonial America, canopies were suspended from the ceiling around a bed. In England around 1560, bedposts were extended to support these heavy canopies, which were draped over simple wooden frames attached to the extended bedposts. During the summer, lighter material kept out flying insects. Heavier canopies warded off cold drafts in the winter. Can-

170

opies were also important for privacy, because many people often shared one room.

At first, bedposts were very large and had ornate carvings, but as time passed and styles changed, they became thinner and plainer. In the country, where most craftsmen did not have large long-bed lathes, the octagonal pencil-post bed became very popular. Since most home crafters do not have large long-bed lathes today, this is still a great design. This simple bed can be made easily with tools most woodworkers have available. Its design does not use difficult-to-make mortise-and-tenon joints; rather, it incorporates a method of holding beds together that was used around 1825—cast-iron bed-rail supports. Two sets of eight fasteners are required for each bed.

The dimensions given are designed for either a standard twin-size mattress or a standard queen-size mattress. You can easily change the dimensions to fit any mattress you wish. I have provided various headboards to choose from. You could also make an arched canopy, but I think the flat canopy is more "country" and better suits the plain style of the pencil-post bed.

Since pencil-post beds are very expensive, making your own will pay for this book more than one hundred times. Here in New Hampshire, a soft pine pencil-post bed ranges from $1,300 to $1,700. The bed shown cost me about $200 to make using hardwood, and it took only about twenty hours to complete.

Order the purchased parts as soon as possible so they will not delay the project. It is always helpful to build the bed around the purchased parts.

Step 1. Study the plans carefully, checking the shape of each part. Visualize how you will make the pencil-post bed and what tools you will need. If you have a router, you should buy a 45° cutter bit with a ball-bearing follower.

Step 2. As you study the plans, note the order in which the project is to be assembled.

Step 3. Since the headboard (part 8) has an irregular shape, it should be laid out using a 1-inch grid to make a full-size pattern on heavy paper or cardboard. Transfer the shape of the piece to the grid, and then trace it on the wood.

Step 4. Carefully cut all parts according to the materials list. Cut all parts to exact size and cut the edges exactly square (90°). Recheck all dimensions.

Step 5. Lightly sand all surfaces and edges with medium sandpaper to remove any burrs or tool marks. Keep all edges square and sharp.

Step 6. Follow the detailed illustrations and dimensions for making the parts. Check all dimensions for accuracy. Resand with fine-grit paper, keeping all edges sharp. The posts are laid out and cut with a band saw. The wider the blade you use, the better. I used a ¾-inch-wide blade in my 14-inch Delta band saw. You will have to compound-cut the bed posts; that is, make one long cut and then tape the cut-off piece back on before making the next cut. Make the four long, tapered cuts in each post and plane the surfaces. (A power plane would save time.) The 45° chamfer cut on each edge can be made with a draw knife, or even better, with a router that has a 45° cutter bit and a ball-bearing follower. It will take only a short time for each edge using the router and bit, and you will have a perfect 45° cut along the entire length. (To save time on this project, you can buy a router, bit, and power planer and still be way ahead—and you will have tools for other projects.)

Step 7. To make the mortise cuts of the band rail supports, I used a $1^1/_8$-inch-diameter Forstner bit and drilled a series of holes, $^7/_{16}$ inch deep, the entire length. Note the location of the mortise cut and make all cuts the same—$14^1/_8$ inches from the end and $4^7/_8$ inches long as shown. The bed rail supports are all located nearest the interior edge of each corner; carefully study the top-view detail of the corner before making these cuts. You might want to make a sample corner joint out of scrap wood to test the joint with the cast iron fittings before cutting the bedposts.

Step 8. Carefully lay out the mortise for the headboard; drill a series of holes and chisel out. Check your work as you go so that you do not make any errors in layout.

Step 9. Screw the cast iron, male bed-rail supports to the side and end rails. Screw the female bed-rail supports to the posts; they should be snug in the mortise holes.

Step 10. After all the pieces have been made, dry-fit them; that is, assemble the complete project without glue or nails to check for accuracy and joint fit. If any parts fit poorly, now is the time to make corrections. Note that the headboards are not glued or pinned in place; rather, they are allowed to "float" in the mortise holes in the posts. The end rails (part 5) will keep them in place. Glue and screw the supports (part 3) to the side rails (part 2) as shown.

Step 11. If all parts fit together well, keep them assembled and finish the project at this point. This will allow you to apply the finish and support pieces while they are air-drying. Finish to suit, using the general finishing instructions.

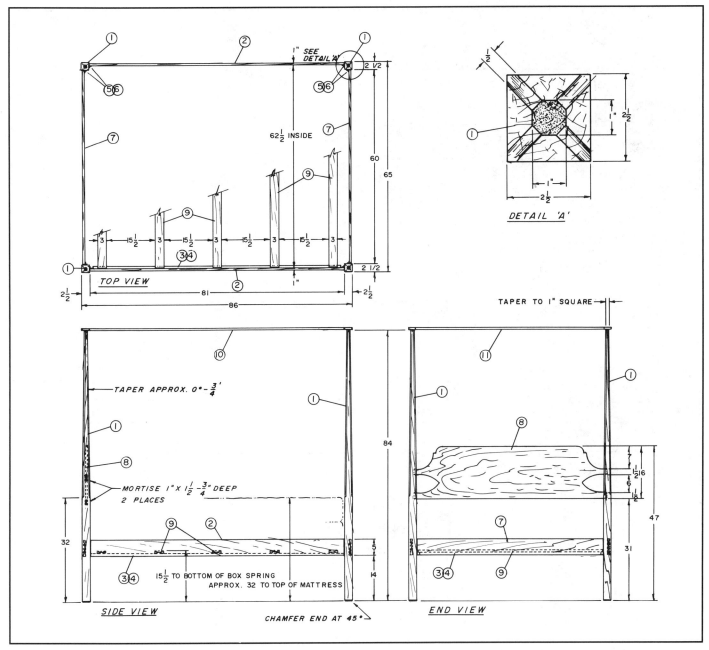

Queen bed

	PART	INCHES	NEEDED
1	POST	$2^{1}/_{2} \times 2^{1}/_{2} \times 84$	4
2	SIDE RAIL	$1 \times 5 \times 81$	2
3	SUPPORT	$^{3}/_{4} \times ^{3}/_{4} \times 80$	2
4	FLAT-HEAD SCREW	NO. 8—$1^{1}/_{2}$	20
5	END RAIL	$1 \times 5 \times 60$	2
6	BED RAIL FASTENER	NO. 6000 OR EQUAL	2 SETS
7	FLAT-HEAD SCREW	NO. 8—$^{7}/_{8}$	20
8	HEADBOARD	$1 \times 16 \times 61^{1}/_{2}$	1
9	BOX SPRING SUPPORT	$^{3}/_{4} \times 3 \times 62^{7}/_{16}$	5
10	TESTER RAIL	$^{3}/_{4} \times 1^{1}/_{2} \times 85$	2
11	TESTER RAIL	$^{3}/_{4} \times 1^{1}/_{2} \times 64$	2

173

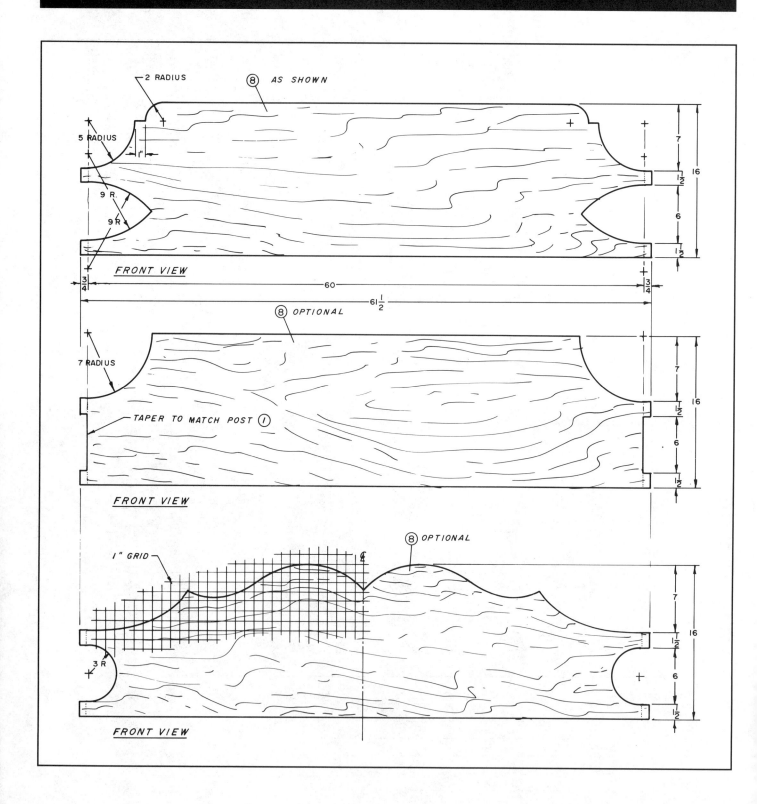

2 RADIUS

⑧ AS SHOWN

5 RADIUS

9 R.

9 R

FRONT VIEW

3/4

60

61 1/2

7

1 1/2

6

1 1/2

16

3/4

⑧ *OPTIONAL*

7 RADIUS

TAPER TO MATCH POST ①

FRONT VIEW

7

1 1/2

6

1 1/2

16

⑧ *OPTIONAL*

1" GRID

3 R

FRONT VIEW

7

1 1/2

6

1 1/2

16

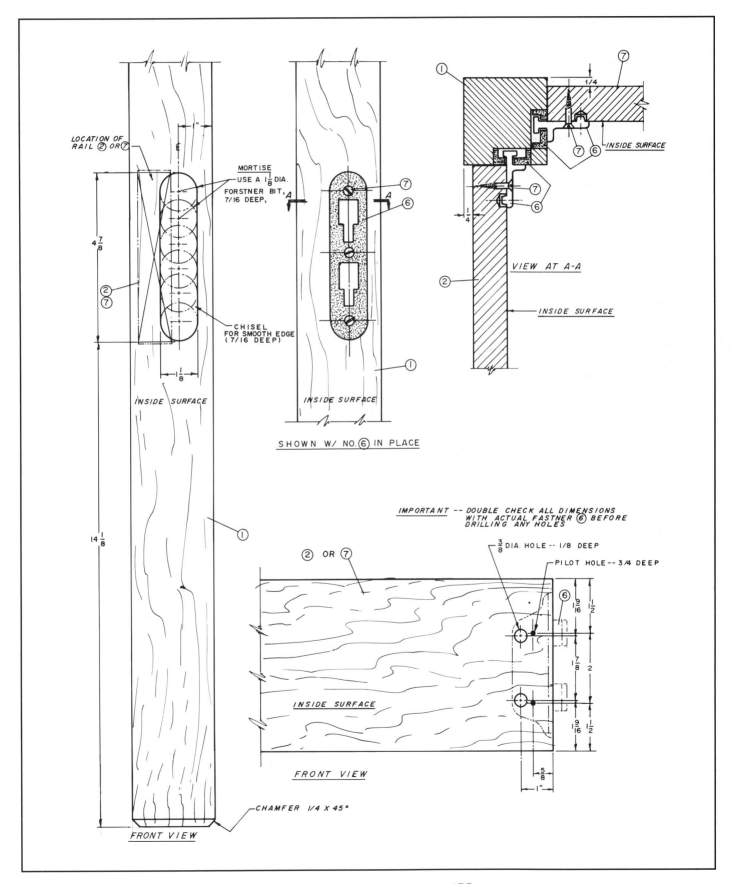

LOCATION OF RAIL ② OR ⑦

MORTISE
USE A 1 1/8 DIA.
FORSTNER BIT,
7/16 DEEP,

CHISEL
FOR SMOOTH EDGE
(7/16 DEEP)

4 7/8

②
⑦

1 1/8

INSIDE SURFACE

14 1/8

①

CHAMFER 1/4 X 45°

FRONT VIEW

SHOWN W/ NO. ⑥ IN PLACE

INSIDE SURFACE

⑦
⑥

①

VIEW AT A-A

①
⑦
1/4

⑦
⑥
INSIDE SURFACE

②
⑦
⑥

1/4

②

INSIDE SURFACE

IMPORTANT -- DOUBLE CHECK ALL DIMENSIONS
WITH ACTUAL FASTNER ⑥ BEFORE
DRILLING ANY HOLES

② OR ⑦

3/8 DIA. HOLE -- 1/8 DEEP

PILOT HOLE -- 3/4 DEEP

⑥

9/16
1 1/2

7/8
2

INSIDE SURFACE

1 9/16
1 1/2

5/8
1"

FRONT VIEW

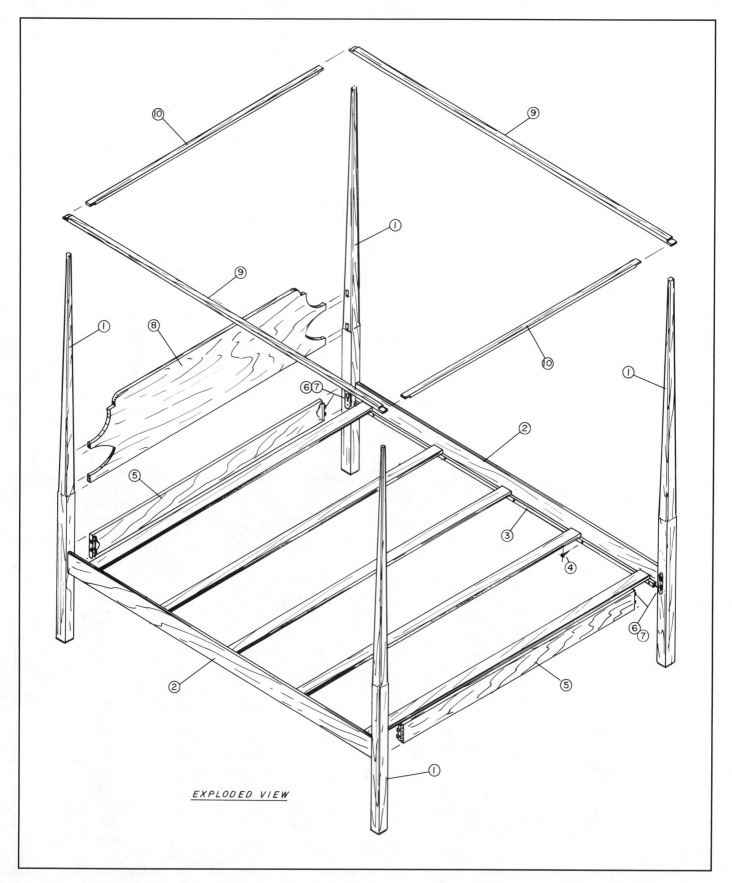

EXPLODED VIEW

176

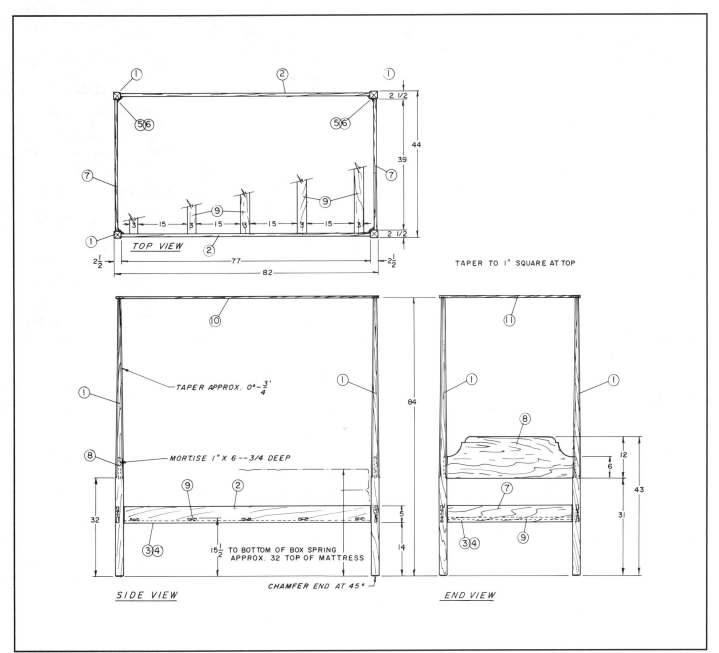

Twin bed

PART		INCHES	NEEDED
1	POST	$2\frac{1}{2} \times 2\frac{1}{2} \times 84$	4
2	SIDE RAIL	$1 \times 5 \times 77$	2
3	SUPPORT	$\frac{3}{4} \times \frac{3}{4} \times 76$	2
4	FLAT-HEAD SCREW	NO. 8—$1\frac{1}{2}$	20
5	END RAIL	$1 \times 5 \times 39$	2
6	BED RAIL FASTENER	NO. 6000 OR EQUAL	2 SETS
7	FLAT-HEAD SCREW	NO. 8—$\frac{7}{8}$	20
8	HEADBOARD	$1 \times 12 \times 40\frac{1}{2}$	1
9	BOX SPRING SUPPORT	$\frac{3}{4} \times 3 \times 41\frac{7}{16}$	5
10	TESTER RAIL	$\frac{3}{4} \times 1\frac{1}{2} \times 81$	2
11	TESTER RAIL	$\frac{3}{4} \times 1\frac{1}{2} \times 43$	2

Metric Equivalents

INCHES TO MILLIMETRES

IN.	MM	IN.	MM
1	25.4	51	1295.4
2	50.8	52	1320.8
3	76.2	53	1346.2
4	101.6	54	1371.6
5	127.0	55	1397.0
6	152.4	56	1422.4
7	177.8	57	1447.8
8	203.2	58	1473.2
9	228.6	59	1498.6
10	254.0	60	1524.0
11	279.4	61	1549.4
12	304.8	62	1574.8
13	330.2	63	1600.2
14	355.6	64	1625.6
15	381.0	65	1651.0
16	406.4	66	1676.4
17	431.8	67	1701.8
18	457.2	68	1727.2
19	482.6	69	1752.6
20	508.0	70	1778.0
21	533.4	71	1803.4
22	558.8	72	1828.8
23	584.2	73	1854.2
24	609.6	74	1879.6
25	635.0	75	1905.0
26	660.4	76	1930.4
27	685.8	77	1955.8
28	711.2	78	1981.2
29	736.6	79	2006.6
30	762.0	80	2032.0
31	787.4	81	2057.4
32	812.8	82	2082.8
33	838.2	83	2108.2
34	863.6	84	2133.6
35	889.0	85	2159.0
36	914.4	86	2184.4
37	939.8	87	2209.8
38	965.2	88	2235.2
39	990.6	89	2260.6
40	1016.0	90	2286.0
41	1041.4	91	2311.4
42	1066.8	92	2336.8
43	1092.2	93	2362.2
44	1117.6	94	2387.6
45	1143.0	95	2413.0
46	1168.4	96	2438.4
47	1193.8	97	2463.8
48	1219.2	98	2489.2
49	1244.6	99	2514.6
50	1270.0	100	2540.0

The above table is exact on the basis: 1 in. = 25.4 mm

U.S. TO METRIC
1 inch = 2.540 centimetres
1 foot = .305 metre
1 yard = .914 metre
1 mile = 1.609 kilometres

METRIC TO U.S.
1 millimetre = .039 inch
1 centimetre = .394 inch
1 metre = 3.281 feet or 1.094 yards
1 kilometre = .621 mile

INCH-METRIC EQUIVALENTS

FRACTION	DECIMAL EQUIVALENT CUSTOMARY (IN.)	METRIC (MM)	FRACTION	DECIMAL EQUIVALENT CUSTOMARY (IN.)	METRIC (MM)
1/64	.015	0.3969	33/64	.515	13.0969
1/32	.031	0.7938	17/32	.531	13.4938
3/64	.046	1.1906	35/64	.546	13.8906
1/16	.062	1.5875	9/16	.562	14.2875
5/64	.078	1.9844	37/64	.578	14.6844
3/32	.093	2.3813	19/32	.593	15.0813
7/64	.109	2.7781	39/64	.609	15.4781
1/8	.125	3.1750	5/8	.625	15.8750
9/64	.140	3.5719	41/64	.640	16.2719
5/32	.156	3.9688	21/32	.656	16.6688
11/64	.171	4.3656	43/64	.671	17.0656
3/16	.187	4.7625	11/16	.687	17.4625
13/64	.203	5.1594	45/64	.703	17.8594
7/32	.218	5.5563	23/32	.718	18.2563
15/64	.234	5.9531	47/64	.734	18.6531
1/4	.250	6.3500	3/4	.750	19.0500
17/64	.265	6.7469	49/64	.765	19.4469
9/32	.281	7.1438	25/32	.781	19.8438
19/64	.296	7.5406	51/64	.796	20.2406
5/16	.312	7.9375	13/16	.812	20.6375
21/64	.328	8.3384	53/64	.828	21.0344
11/32	.343	8.7313	27/32	.843	21.4313
23/64	.359	9.1281	55/64	.859	21.8281
3/8	.375	9.5250	7/8	.875	22.2250
25/64	.390	9.9219	57/64	.890	22.6219
13/32	.406	10.3188	29/32	.906	23.0188
27/64	.421	10.7156	59/64	.921	23.4156
7/16	.437	11.1125	15/16	.937	23.8125
29/64	.453	11.5094	61/64	.953	24.2094
15/32	.468	11.9063	31/32	.968	24.6063
31/64	.484	12.3031	63/64	.984	25.0031
1/2	.500	12.7000	1	1.000	25.4000

Appendixes

SUPPLIERS

The following is a list of sources for various woodworking-related products that will be helpful in completing the projects in this book. The list is by no means complete. Although some catalogs are free, others range from $1 to $4. Write for more information.

BEVELED GLASS

Beveled Glass Works
11721 S.E. Taylor
Portland, OR 97216

Floral Glass and Mirror
Mirror Division
895 Motor Parkway
Hauppauge, NY 11788

**MEASURED DRAWINGS
OF ANTIQUES**

John A. Nelson
220 General Miller Rd.
Peterborough, NH 03458

PAINT

Cohasset Colonials
Cohasset, MA 02025

Industrial Finishing Products
465 Logan St.
Brooklyn, NY 11208

Stulb Paint and Chemical Co., Inc.
P.O. Box 297
Norristown, PA 19404

The Wise Co.
6503 St. Claude Ave.
P.O. Box 118
Arabi, LA 70032

Wood Finishing Supply Co.
100 Throop St.
Palmyra, NY 14522

MILK PAINT

The Old Fashioned Milk Paint Co.
Main St.
Groton, MA 01450

STAINS, TUNG OIL

Behlem's (Mohawk Finishes)
Route 30 N. Amsterdam
New York, NY 12010

Cohasset Colonials
Cohasset, MA 02025

Deft, Inc.
17451 Von Darman Ave.
Irvine, CA 92714

Minwax
15 Mercedes Dr.
Montvale, NJ 07645

The McClosky Corp.
7600 State Rd.
Philadelphia, PA 19136

Thompson and Formby's, Inc.
825 Crossover La., Ste. 240
Memphis, TN 38117

Olympic Stain
2233 112th Ave. N.E.
Bellevue, WA 98004

Pratt and Lambert Specialty Products
P.O. Box 1505
Buffalo, NY 14240

Stulb Paint and Chemical Co., Inc.
P.O. Box 297
Norristown, PA 19404

Watco-Dennis Corp.
Michigan Ave. and 22nd St.
Santa Monica, CA 90404

**FINISHERS FOR EATING
UTENSILS**

Woodcraft Supply (Behlem's Salad Bowl
Finish)
41 Atlantic Ave.
P.O. Box 4000
Woburn, MA 01888

Constantine's (Preserve Woodenware Oil)
2050 Eastchester Rd.
Bronx, NY 10461

PAINT FOR CHILDREN'S TOYS

Garrett Wade (Shellac flakes and ethyl
alcohol solvent)
161 Avenue of the Americas
New York, NY 10013

179

Meisel Hardware Specialties (Special paint and hardware)
P.O. Box 70
Mound, MN 55364-0070

Cherry Tree Toys (Craft and tole paint)
P.O. Box 369
Belmont, OH 43718

OLD-FASHIONED NAILS, BRASS SCREWS

DRI Industries
11300 Hampshire Ave. S.
Bloomington, MN 55438

Elwick Supply Co.
230 Woods La.
Somerdale, NJ 08083

Equality Screw Co., Inc.
P.O. Box 1296
El Cajon, CA 92002

Morton Brasses
P.O. Box 95
Nooks Hill Rd.
Cromwell, CT 06416

The Nutty Co.
P.O. Box 473
Derby, CT 06418

Tremont Nail Co.
P.O. Box 111
21 Elm St.
Wareham, MA 02571

BRASSES

Armor Products
P.O. Box 445-H
East Northport, NY 11731

Ball and Ball
463 W. Lincoln Hwy.
Exton, PA 19341

A Carolina Craftsman
975 S. Avacado St.
Anaheim, CA 92805

The Brass Tree
308 N. Main St.
Charles, MO 63301

Garrett Wade Co., Inc.
161 Avenue of the Americas
New York, NY 10013

Heirloom Antiques Brass Co.
P.O. Box 146
Dundass, MN 55019

Horton Brasses
P.O. Box 95
Nooks Hill Rd.
Cromwell, CT 06416

Imported European Hardware
4295 S. Arville
Las Vegas, NV 89103

Mason and Sullivan Co.
586 Higgins Crowell Rd.
West Yarmouth, MA 02678

18th Century Hardware Co., Inc.
131 E. Third St.
Derry, PA 15627

Period Furniture Hardware Co.
123 Charles St.
Box 314
Charles St. Station
Boston, MA 02114

19th-Century Hardware Supply
P.O. Box 599
Rough and Ready, CA 95975

Paxton Hardware, Ltd.
7818 Bradshaw Rd.
Upper Falls, MD 21156

The Renovators' Supply
6254 Renovators' Old Mill
Millers Falls, MA 01349

The Shop, Inc.
P.O. Box 3711
RD 3
Reading, PA 19606

Ritter and Son Hardware
Dept. WJ
Gualala, CA 95445

Woodbury Blacksmith and Forge Co.
P.O. Box 268
Woodbury, CT 06798

DRAFTING SUPPLIES

Modern School Supplies
P.O. Box 958
Hartford, CT 06143

CUSTOM TURNINGS

Riverbend Turnings
RD 1
P.O. Box 364
Wellsville, NY 14895

QUEEN ANNE LEGS

Adams Wood Products, Inc.
974 Forest Dr.
Morristown, TN 37814

FINE WOOD

Berea Hardwoods Co.
125 Jacqueline Dr.
Berea, OH 44017

Craft Woods
10921 York Rd.
Cockeysville, MD 21030

Croffwood Mills
RD 1, Box 14
Driftwood, PA 15832

Hardwoods of Memphis
P.O. Box 12449
Memphis, TN 38182

Manny's Woodworking Pl.
602 S. Broadway
Lexington, KY 40508

Northeast Hardwoods
P.O. Box 365
Salamanca, NY 14770

Paxton Beautiful Woods
P.O. Box 407171
5420 S. 99th East Ave.
Tulsa, OK 74147-0171

Woodcrafters of Spring Green Wisconsin
P.O. Box 566
Spring Green, WI 53588

VENEERING

Bob Morgan Woodworking Supplies
1123 Bardstown Rd.
Louisville, KY 40204

GENERAL CATALOGS

Brookstone Co.
Vose Farm Rd.
Peterborough, NH 03458

Cherry Tree Toys Corp.
P.O. Box 369
Belmont, OH 43718

Crafter's Mart
P.O. Box 2342
Greely, CO 80632

Craftsman Wood Service Co.
1735 W. Cortland Ct.
Addison, IL 60101

Constantine
2050 Eastchester Rd.
Bronx, NY 10461

Cryder Creek Wood Shoppe, Inc.
P.O. Box 19
Whitesville, NY 14897

The Fine Tool Shops
P.O. Box 1262
20 Backus Ave.
Danbury, CT 06810

Geneva Specialties
P.O. Box 636
Lake Geneva, WI 53147

Garrett Wade Co., Inc.
161 Avenue of the Americas
New York, NY 10013

Leichtung, Inc.
4944 Commerce Pkwy.
Cleveland, OH 44128

Meisel Hardware Specialties
P.O. Box 70
Mound, MN 55364

R.J.S. Custom Woodworking
P.O. Box 12354
Kansas City, KS 66112

Silvo Hardware Co.
2205 Richmond St.
Philadelphia, PA 19125

Trendlines
375 Beacham St.
Chelsea, MA 02150

Woodcraft Supply
P.O. Box 4000
41 Atlantic Ave.
Woburn, MA 01888

Woodworks
P.O. Box 14507
Ft. Worth, TX 76117

Woodworkers Supply of New Mexico
5604 Alameda, N.E.
Albuquerque, NM 87113

CLOCK SUPPLIES

The American Clockmaker
P.O. Box 326
Clintonville, WI 54929

Armor Products
P.O. Box 445
East Northport, NY 11731

Cas-Ker Co.
2121 Sprint Grove Ave.
Cincinnati, OH 45214

Emperor Clock Co.
Emperor Industrial Park
Fairhope, AL 36532

H. DeCounick & Son
P.O. Box 68
200 Market Plaza
Alamo, CA 94507

Klockit
P.O. Box 636
Lake Geneva, WI 53147

S. LaRose, Inc.
234 Commerce Pl.
Greensboro, NC 27420

Mason and Sullivan Co.
586 Higgins Crowell Rd.
West Yarmouth, MA 02678

Merritt's Antiques, Inc.
Rt. 2
Douglassville, PA 19518

Newport Enterprises
2313 West Burbank Blvd.
Burbank, CA 91506

Turncraft, Inc.
825 Boone Ave.
Golden Valley, MN 54276

STENCILING SUPPLIES

Adelle Bishop, Inc.
Dorset, VT 05251

Creative Arts & Crafts, Inc.
P.O. Box 11491
Knoxville, TN 37939-1491

ROUTERBITS

Cascade Tools, Inc.
P.O. Box 3110
Bellingham, MA 98225

FURNITURE KITS SUPPLIERS

In most cases, these kits come precut, presanded, and ready to assemble. They usually require only a minimum of tools.

The Bartley Collection, Ltd.
3 Airpark Dr., Dept. 4662
Easton, MD 21601
Antique reproduction furniture kits, ranging from a pipe box to a Newport chest and a Queen Anne highboy.

Cohasset Colonials
830 Ship St.
Cohasset, MA 02025
Large variety of Colonial-style furniture and reproductions.

Craftsman's Corner
P.O. Box AP
4012 N.E. 14th St.
Des Moines, IA 50302
Broad range of solid oak furniture and accessory kits, from clocks and magazine racks to rolltop desks, file cabinets, tables, and chairs.

Shaker Workshops
P.O. Box 1028
Concord, MA 01742
Reproductions of Shaker furniture and accessories, ranging from simple oval boxes to chairs, beds, and tables.

Yield House
Rt. 16
North Conway, NH 03860
Antique reproductions and country pieces, from towel racks and wall shelves to armoires and entertainment centers.

SCHOOLS AND CRAFT CENTERS

The following are instructional programs available to woodworkers. Each school has a variety of short- and long-term programs, ranging from one-day seminars to full undergraduate and graduate degree programs. Write for information. I have attended Fletcher Farm School and Brookfield Craft Center and recommend both.

Anderson Ranch Arts Center
Snowmass Village, CO 81615
One- and two-week summer workshops in furniture design and woodworking.

Arrowmont School of Arts and Crafts
P.O. Box 567
Gatlinburg, TN 37738
One- and two-week classes in woodturning in March, June, July, and August. One class in wood construction in June.

Brookfield Craft Center
P.O. Box 122
Brookfield, CT 06804
One- or two-day weekend workshops in all areas of woodworking and wood carving. Week-long workshops in summer.

College of the Redwoods
440 Alger St.
Fort Bragg, CA 95437
James Krenov offers a nine-month program in fine cabinetmaking.

Country Workshops
90 Mill Creek Rd.
Marshall, NC 28735
Five- and six-day workshops and seminars on a wide range of woodworking topics. Courses given in alternate weeks during summer.

Fletcher Farm School for the Arts and Crafts
RR #1, Box 1041
Ludlow, VT 05149
Summer classes in Early American arts and crafts, weekly and on weekends.

Haystack Mountain School of Crafts
Deer Isle, ME 04627
Summer sessions in a variety of woodworking and craft topics. Five two- or three-week courses.

James L. Cox Woodworking School
RD 2, Box 126
Honey Brook, PA 19344
Two-day courses in woodturning offered to one or two students at a time.

North Bennett Street School
39 N. Bennett St.
Boston, MA 02113
Degree program in woodworking.

Olde Mille Cabinet Shoppe
RD 3, Box 547A
York, PA 17402
Weekend seminars and workshops held throughout the year.

Oregon School of Arts and Crafts
8245 S.W. Barnes Rd.
Portland, OR 97225
Summer programs, workshops, and three-year certificate program (BFA degree available through affiliated university).

Penland School
Penland, NC 28765-0037
One-, two-, and three-week courses in general woodworking during the summer. Courses for credit available during the fall.

Peters Valley Crafts Center
Layton, NJ 07851
One- to nine-day summer workshops in woodworking. Topics include dovetailed boxes, curved doors, and veneering.

Rhode Island School of Design
2 College St.
Providence, RI 03903

Undergraduate courses in furniture design and woodworking and graduate degree in furniture design. Evening and weekend courses in basic woodworking also available for credit or noncredit.

Rochester Institute of Technology, School for American Craftsmen,
College of Fine and Applied Arts
1 Lomb Memorial Dr.
Rochester, NY 14623

Two-year program in furniture design and woodworking. Intensive apprentice program that offers associate degree.

Southeastern Massachusetts University College of Visual and Performing Arts (formerly Swain School of Design)
1213 Purchase St.
New Bedford, MA 02740

Undergraduate and graduate program in woodworking and furniture design. Also continuing education courses in woodworking.

Vermont State Craft Center at Frog Hollow
Middlebury, VT 05753

Night and weekend courses in woodworking.

Worcester Craft Center
25 Sagamore Rd.
Worcester, MA 01605

Full range of woodworking programs, from two-year full-time study to continuing education courses to children's woodworking classes. Courses run fall, spring, and five weeks during the summer. Prominent woodworkers also hold workshops.

RELATED PUBLICATIONS

American Woodworker
33 E. Minor St.
Emmaus, PA 18098

Early American Life
P.O. Box 8200
Harrisburg, PA 17105

Fine Woodworking
The Taunton Press
P.O. Box 355
52 Church Hill Rd.
Newton, CT 06470

International Woodworking Magazine
Plymouth, NH 03264

Popular Woodworker
EGW Publishing Co.
1300 Galaxy Way
Concord, CA 94520

Wood
P.O. Box 10625
Des Moines, IA 50380-0625

Woodsmith
2200 Grand Ave.
Des Moines, IA 50312

The Woodworkers Journal
P.O. Box 1629
517 Litchfield Rd.
New Milford, CT 06776

Workbench Magazine
P.O. Box 5965
Kansas City, MO 64110

Woodwork Magazine
P.O. Box 1929
Ross, CA 94957

WOODWORKING ASSOCIATIONS, CLUBS, AND GUILDS

Alabama Woodworkers Guild
P.O. Box 327
Pelham, AL 35214

Alaska Creative Woodworkers
Greg Motyka
2136 Alder Dr.
Anchorage, AK 99508

Augusta Woodworkers Guild
P.O. Box 15
Augusta, MO 63332

Baulines Craftsman Guild
55 Sunnyside
Mill Valley, CA 94941

Green Country Woodworkers Club
P.O. Box 470856
Tulsa, OK 74147-0856

Guild of Oregon Woodworkers
P.O. Box 1866
Portland, OR 97207

Inland Empire Woodworkers Guild
P.O. Box 7413
Spokane, WA 99207

Kansas City Woodworkers Guild
510 N. Sterling
Sugar Creek, MO 64054

Michigan Woodworkers Guild
P.O. Box 7802
Ann Arbor, MI 48107

Midwest Woodworkers Association
Gerald Jones
311 Cumberland Rd.
Columbia, MO 65203

North Texas Woodworkers Guild
P.O. Box 224886
Dallas, TX 75222

Society of Philadelphia Woodworkers
c/o Chestnut Hill Academy
500 W. Willow Grove Ave.
Philadelphia, PA 19118

Souris Valley Woodworkers Association
P.O. Box 3042
Minot, ND 58702

Southeast American Craft Council
Art Dept.
Longwood College
Farmville, VA 23901

Vancouver Island Woodworkers Guild
Box 6584, Station C
Victoria, British Columbia
Canada V8P 5N7

Virginia Mountain Crafts Guild
P.O. Box 1001
Salem, VA 24153

Wisconsin Woodworkers Guild
Jim Lingle, President
P.O. Box 137
Milwaukee, WI 53201

Woodworkers Association of
North America
P.O. Box 706
Plymouth, NH 03264

Woodworkers Association of Topeka
Cleo McDonald, President
9421 N.W. 42nd St.
Silver Lake, KS 66539

Woodworkers Guild of Georgia
P.O. Box 1113
Conyers, GA 30207

Woodwrights Gallery
P.O. Box 7571
Klamath Falls, OR 97602

FOR FURTHER STUDY

The following list includes places where antique furniture can be found and studied. It is a good idea to write any place you wish to visit to find out the visiting hours.

American Clock and Watch Museum
100 Maple St.
Bristol, CT 06010

Bennington Museum
W. Main St.
Bennington, VT 05201

Boston Museum of Fine Arts
465 Huntington Ave.
Boston, MA 02115

Colonial Williamsburg
P.O. Box C
Williamsburg, VA 23187

Farmers' Museum
P.O. Box 800
Lake Road
Cooperstown, NY 13326

Hancock Shaker Village
P.O. Box 898, Rt. 20
Pittsfield, MA 01202

Henry Ford Museum and
  Greenfield Village
P.O. Box 1970
Dearborn, MI 48121

Index of American Design
6th and Constitution Ave., N.W.
Washington, DC 20565

Landis Valley Farm Museum
Lancaster, PA 17600

Maritime Museum
2905 Hyde St.
San Francisco, CA 94123

Metropolitan Museum of Art
82d St. and 5th Ave.
New York, NY 10028

Mystic Seaport
P.O. Box 6000
Mystic, CT 06355

National Gallery of Art
Washington, DC 20565

Old Deerfield Village
Deerfield, MA 01342

Old Salem
Drawer F
Winston-Salem, NC 27108

Old Sturbridge Village
1 Old Sturbridge Village Rd.
Sturbridge, MA 01566-0200

Philadelphia Museum of Art
P.O. Box 7646
Philadelphia, PA 19101-7646

Plimoth Plantation
P.O. Box 1620
Warren Ave.
Plymouth, MA 02360

Salem Harbor
54 Turner St.
Salem, MA 01970

Saugus Iron Works
244 Central St.
Saugus, MA 01906

Shelburne Museum
Rt. 7
Shelburne, VT 05401

Smithsonian Institution
10th and Constitution, N.W.
Washington, DC 20560

Strawberry Banke Museum
P.O. Box 300
454 Court St.
Portsmouth, NH 03801

Thomas Lee House
Old Lyme, CT 06371

Wenham Museum
132 Main St., Rt., 1A
Wenham, MA 01984